The

Mary McNeil Fenollosa

Alpha Editions

This edition published in 2021

ISBN : 9789355342669

Design and Setting By
Alpha Editions
www.alphaedis.com
Email - info@alphaedis.com

As per information held with us this book is in Public Domain. This book is a reproduction of an important historical work. Alpha Editions uses the best technology to reproduce historical work in the same manner it was first published to preserve its original nature. Any marks or number seen are left intentionally to preserve its true form.

I

The old folks call it Yeddo. To the young, "Tokyo" has a pleasant, modern sound, and comes glibly. But whether young or old, those whose home it is know that the great flat city, troubled with green hills, cleft by a shining river, and veined in living canals, is the central spot of all the world.

Storms visit Tokyo,—with fury often, sometimes with destruction. Earthquakes cow it; snow falls upon its temple roofs, swings in wet, dazzling masses from the bamboo plumes, or balances in white strata along green-black pine branches. The summer sun scorches the face of Yeddo, and summer rain comes down in wide bands of light. With evening the mist creeps up, thrown over it like a covering, casting a spell of silence through which the yellow lanterns of the hurrying jinrikishas dance an elfish dance, and the voices of the singing-girls pierce like fine blades of sound.

But to know the full charm of the great city, one must wake with it at some rebirth of dawn. This hour gives to the imaginative in every land a thrill, a yearning, and a pang of visual regeneration. In no place is this wonder more deeply touched with mystery than in modern Tokyo.

Far off to the east the Sumida River lies in sleep. Beyond it, temple roofs—black keels of sunken vessels—cut a sky still powdered thick with stars. Nothing moves, and yet a something changes! The darkness shivers as to a cold touch. A pallid haze breathes wanly on the surface of the impassive sky. The gold deepens swiftly and turns to a faint rose flush. The stars scamper away like mice.

Across the moor of gray house eaves the mist wavers. Day troubles it. A pink light rises to the zenith, and the mist shifts and slips away in layers, pink and gold and white. Now far beyond the grayness, to the west, the cone of Fuji flashes into splendor. It, too, is pink. Its shape is of a lotos bud, and the long fissures that plough a mountain side are now but delicate gold veining on a petal. Slowly it seems to open. It is the chalice of a new day, the signal and the pledge of consecration. Husky crows awake in the pine trees, and doves under the temple eaves. The east is red beyond the river, and the round, red sun, insignia of this land, soars up like a cry of triumph.

On the glittering road of the Sumida, loaded barges, covered for the night with huge squares of fringed straw mats, begin to nod and preen themselves like a covey of gigantic river birds. Sounds of prayer and of silver matin bells come from the temples, where priest and acolyte greet the

Lord Buddha of a new day. From tiny chimneyless kitchens of a thousand homes thin blue feathers of smoke make slow upward progress, to be lost in the last echoes of the vanishing mist. Sparrows begin to chirp, first one, then ten, then thousands. Their voices have the clash and chime of a myriad small triangles.

The wooden outer panels (amado) of countless dwellings are thrust noisily aside and stacked into a shallow closet. The noise reverberates from district to district in a sharp musketry of sound. Maid servants call cheerily across bamboo fences. Shoji next are opened, disclosing often the dull green mosquito net hung from corner to corner of the low-ceiled sleeping rooms. Children, in brilliant night robes, run to the verandas to see the early sun; cocks strut in pigmy gardens. Now, from along the streets rise the calls of flower peddlers, of venders of fish, bean-curd, vegetables, and milk. Thus the day comes to modern Tokyo, which the old folks still call Yeddo.

On such a midsummer dawn, not many years ago, old Kano Indara, sleeping in his darkened chamber, felt the summons of an approaching joy. Beauty tugged at his dreams. Smiling, as a child that is led by love, he rose, drew aside softly the shoji, then the amado of his room, and then, with face uplifted, stepped down into his garden. The beauty of the ebbing night caught at his sleeve, but the dawn held him back.

It was the moment just before the great Sun took place upon his throne. Kano still felt himself lord of the green space round about him. On their pretty bamboo trellises the potted morning-glory vines held out flowers as yet unopened. They were fragile, as if of tissue, and were beaded at the crinkled tips with dew. Kano's eyelids, too, had dew of tears upon them. He crouched close to the flowers. Something in him, too, some new ecstacy was to unfurl. His lean body began to tremble. He seated himself at the edge of the narrow, railless veranda along which the growing plants were ranged. One trembling bud reached out as if it wished to touch him.

The old man shook with the beating of his own heart. He was an artist. Could he endure another revelation of joy? Yes, his soul, renewed ever as the gods themselves renew their youth, was to be given the inner vision. Now, to him, this was the first morning. Creation bore down upon him.

The flower, too, had begun to tremble. Kano turned directly to it. The filmy, azure angles at the tip were straining to part, held together by just one drop of light. Even as Kano stared the drop fell heavily, plashing on his hand. The flower, with a little sob, opened to him, and questioned him of life, of art, of immortality. The old man covered his face, weeping.

The last of his race was Kano Indara; the last of a mighty line of artists. Even in this material age his fame spread as the mists of his own land, and his name was known in barbarian countries far across the sea. Tokyo might fall under the blight of progress, but Kano would hold to the traditions of his race. To live as a true artist,—to die as one,—this was his care. He might have claimed high position in the great Art Museum recently inaugurated by the new government, and housed in an abomination of pink stucco with Moorish towers at the four corners. He might even have been elected president of the new Academy, and have presided over the Italian sculptors and degenerate French painters imported to instruct and "civilize" modern Japan. Stiff graphite pencils, making lines as hard and sharp as those in the faces of foreigners themselves, were to take the place of the soft charcoal flake whose stroke was of satin and young leaves. Horrible brushes, fashioned of the hair of swine, pinched in by metal bands, and wielded with a hard tapering stick of varnished wood, were to be thrust into the hands of artists,—yes,—artists—men who, from childhood, had known the soft pliant Japanese brush almost as a spirit hand;—had felt the joy of the long stroke down fibrous paper where the very thickening and thinning of the line, the turn of the brush here, the easing of it there, made visual music,—men who had realized the brush as part not only of the body but of the soul,—such men, indeed,—such artists, were to be offered a bunch of hog bristles, set in foreign tin. Why, even in the annals of Kano's own family more than one faithful brush had acquired a soul of its own, and after the master's death had gone on lamenting in his written name. But the foreigners' brushes, and their little tubes of ill-smelling gum colored with dead hues! Kano shuddered anew at the thought.

Naturally he hated all new forms of government. He regretted and deplored the magnanimity of his Emperor in giving to his people, so soon, a modern constitution. What need had Art of a constitution?

Across the northern end of Yeddo runs the green welt of a table-land. Midway, at the base of this, tucked away from northern winds, hidden in green bamboo hedges, Kano lived, a mute protest against the new. Beside himself, of the household were Umè-ko, his only child, and an old family servant, Mata.

Kano's garden, always the most important part of a Japanese dwelling place, ran out in one continuous, shallow terrace to the south. A stone wall upheld its front edge from the narrow street; and on top of this wall stiff hedges grew. In one corner, however, a hillock had been raised, a "Moon Viewing Place," such as poets and artists have always found necessary. From its flat top old Kano had watched through many years the rising of the moon; had seen, as now, a new dawn possess a new-created earth,—

had traced the outlines of the stars. By day he sometimes loved to watch the little street below, delighting in the motion and color of passing groups.

For the garden, itself, it was fashioned chiefly of sand, pebbles, stones, and many varieties of pine, the old artist's favorite plant. A small rock-bound pond curved about the inner base of the moon-viewing hill, duplicating in its clear surface the beauties near. A few splendid carp, the color themselves of dawn, swam lazily about with noses in the direction of the house whence came, they well knew, liberal offerings of rice and cake.

Kano had his plum trees, too; the classic "umè," loved of all artists, poets, and decent-minded people generally. One tree, a superb specimen of the kind called "Crouching-Dragon-Plum," writhed and twisted near the veranda of the chamber of its name-child, Umè-ko, thrusting one leafy arm almost to the paper shoji of her wall. Kano's transient flowers were grown, for the most part in pots, and these his daughter Umè-ko loved to tend. There were morning-glories for the mid-summer season, peonies and iris for the spring, and chrysanthemums for autumn. One foreign rose-plant, pink of bloom, in a blue-gray jar, had been pruned and trained into a beauty that no western rose-bush ever knew.

Behind the Kano cottage the rise of ground for twenty yards was of a grade scarcely perceptible to the eye. Here Mata did the family washing; dried daikon in winter, and sweet-potato slices in the summer sun. This small space she considered her special domain, and was at no pains to conceal the fact. Beyond, the hill went upward suddenly with the curve of a cresting wave. Higher it rose and higher, bearing a tangled growth of vines and ferns and bamboo grass; higher and higher, until it broke, in sheer mid-air, with a coarse foam of rock, thick shrubs, and stony ledges. Almost at the zenith of the cottage garden it poised, and a great camphor tree, centuries old, soared out into the blue like a green balloon.

Behind the camphor tree, again, and not visible from the garden below, stood a temple of the "Shingon" sect, the most mystic of the old esoteric Buddhist forms. To the rear of this the broad, low, rectangular buildings of a nunnery, gray and old as the temple itself brooded among high hedges of the sacred mochi tree. This retreat had been famous for centuries throughout Japan. More than once a Lady Abbess had been yielded from the Imperial family. Formerly the temple had owned many koku of rich land; had held feudal sway over rice fields and whole villages, deriving princely revenue. With the restoration of the Emperor to temporal power, some thirty years before the beginning of this story, most of the land had been confiscated; and now, shrunken like the papal power at Rome, the temple claimed, in land, only those acres bounded by its own hedges and stone temple walls. There were the main building itself, silent, impressive in towering majesty; subordinate chapels and dwellings for priests, a huge smoke-stained refectory, the low nunnery in its spreading gardens and, down the northern slope of the hill, the cemetery, a lichen-growth, as it were, of bristling, close-set tombs in gray stone, the splintered regularity broken in places by the tall rounded column of a priest's grave, set in a ring of wooden sotoba. At irregular intervals clusters of giant bamboo trees sprang like green flame from the fissures of gray rock.

Even in humiliation, in comparative poverty, the temple dominated, for miles around, the imagination of the people, and was the great central note of the landscape. The immediate neighborhood was jealously proud of it. Country folk, journeying by the street below, looked up with lips that whispered invocation. Children climbed the long stone steps to play in the temple courtyard, and feed the beautiful tame doves that lived among the carved dragons of the temple eaves.

In that gray cemetery on the further slope Kano's wife, the young mother who died so long ago that Umè-ko could not remember her at all, slept beneath a granite shaft which said, "A Flower having blossomed in the Night, the Halls of the Gods are fragrant." This was the Buddhist kaimyo, or priestly invocation to the spirit of the dead. Of the more personal part of the young mother, her name, age, and the date of her "divine retirement," these were recorded in the household shrine of the Kano cottage, where her "ihai" stood, just behind a little lamp of pure vegetable oil whose light had never yet been suffered to die. Through this shrine, and the daily loving offices required by it, she had never ceased to be a presence in the house. Even in his passionate desire for a son to inherit the name and traditions of his race, old Kano had not been able to endure the thought of a second wife who might wish the shrine removed.

Umè-ko and her father were well known at the temple, and worshipped often before its golden altars. But Mata scorned the ceremony of the older creed. She was a Shinshu, a Protestant. Her sect discarded mysticism as useless, believed in the marriage of priests, and in the abolition of the monastic life, and relied for salvation only on the love and mercy of Amida, the Buddha of Light.

Sometimes at twilight a group of shadowy human figures, gray as the doves themselves, crept out from the nunnery gate, crossed the wide, pebbled courtyard of the temple and stood, for long moments, by the gnarled roots of the camphor tree, staring out across the beauty of the plain of Yeddo; its shining bay a great mirror to the south, and off, on the western horizon, where the last light hung, Fuji, a cone of porphyry, massive against the gold.

For a full hour, now, Kano had delighted in the morning-glories. At intervals he strolled about the garden to touch separately, as if in greeting, each beloved plant. Except for the deepening fervor of the sun he would have kept no note of time. The last shred of mist had vanished. Crows and sparrows were busy with breakfast for their nestlings.

It was, perhaps, the clamor of these feathered parents that, at last, awoke old Mata in her sleeping closet near the kitchen. She turned drowsily. The presence of an unusual light under the shoji brought her to her knees. The amado in the further part of the house were undoubtedly open. Could robbers have come in the night? And were her master and Miss Umè weltering in gore?

She was on her feet now, pushing with shaking fingers at the sliding walls. She peered at first into Umè's room for there, indeed, lay the core of old Mata's heart. A slender figure on the floor stirred slightly and a sound of soft breathing filled the silence. All was well in Umè's room. She knocked then on Kano's fusuma. There was no response. Cautiously she parted them, and met an incoming flood of morning light. The walls were opened. Through the small square pillars of the veranda she could see, as in a frame, old Kano standing in the garden beside the fish-pond. Even as she gazed, incredulous at her own stupidity in sleeping so late, the temple bell above boomed out six slow strokes. Six! Such a thing had never been known. Well, she must be growing old and worthless. She had better fill her sleeve with pebbles and cast herself into the nearest stream. She hurried back, a tempestuous protest in every step.

"Miss Umè,—Umè-ko!" she called. "Ma-a-a! What has come to us both? The Danna San walks about as if he had been awake for hours. And not a cup of tea for him! The honorable fire does not exist. Surely a demon of sleep has bewitched us."

She had entered the girl's room, and now, while speaking, crossed the narrow space to fling wide, first the shoji, and then the outer amado.

Umè moved lazily. Her lacquered pillow, with its bright cushion, rocked as she stirred. "No demon has found me, Mata San," she murmured, smiling. "No demon unless it be you, cruel nurse, who have dragged me back from a heavenly dream."

"Baku devour your dream!" cried Mata. "I say there is no fire beneath the pot!"

Umè sat up now, and smoothed slowly the loops of her shining hair. The yellow morning sun danced into the corners of her room, rioted among the hues of her silken bed coverings, and paused, abashed, as it were, before the delicate beauty of her face.

As Mata scolded, the girl nestled back among her quilts, smiling mischievously. She loved to tease the old dame. "No, nurse," she protested, "that cannot be. The baku feeds on evil dreams alone, and this was not evil. Ah, nurse, it was so sweet a dream——"

"I can give no time to your honorable fooling," cried Mata, in pretended anger. "Have I the arms of a Hundred-Handed Kwannon that I can do all the household work at once? Attire yourself promptly, I entreat: prepare one of the small trays for your august parent, and get out two of the pickled plums from the blue jar."

Umè, with an exaggerated sigh of regret, rose to her feet. Quilt and cushions were pushed into a corner for later airing. Her toilet was swift and simple. To slip the bright-colored sleeping robe from her and toss it to the heaped-up coverlids, don an undergarment of thin white linen and a scant petticoat of blue crepe, draw over them a day robe of blue and white cotton, and tie all in with a sash of brocaded blue and gold,—that was the sum of it. For washing she had a shallow wooden basin on the kitchen veranda, where cold water splashed incessantly from bamboo tubes thrust into the hillside. Hurriedly drying her face and hands on a small towel that hung from a swinging bamboo hoop, she ran into the kitchen to assist the still grumbling Mata.

By this time old Kano had again seated himself at the edge of his veranda. The summer sun grew unpleasantly warm. The morning-glories on their trellises had begun to droop. A little later they would hang, wretched and limp, mere faded scraps of dissolution. Overhead the temple bell struck seven. Kano shuddered at this foreign marking out of hours. A melancholy, intense as had been his former ecstacy, began to enfold his spirit. Perhaps he had waited too long for the simple breakfast; perhaps the recent glory had drained him of vital force. A hopelessness, alike of life and death, rose about him in a tide.

Umè prostrated herself upon the veranda near him. "Good morning, august father. Will you deign to enter now and partake of food?"

Her voice and the morning face she lifted might have won a smile from a stone image. Kano turned sourly. "Why," he thought, "in Shaka's name, could n't she have been a son?"

He rose, however, shaking off his wooden clogs so that they remained upon the path below, and followed Umè to the zashiki, or main room of the house, with the best view of the garden.

The tea was delicious in its first delicate infusion; the pickled plums most stimulating to a morning appetite.

"Rice and fish will soon honorably eventuate," Umè assured him as she went back, smiling, into the kitchen.

Kano pensively lifted a plum upon the point of a toothpick and began nibbling at its wrinkled skin. Yes, why could she not have been a son? As it was, the girl could paint,—paint far better than most women even the famous ones of old. But, after all, no woman painter could be supreme. Love comes first with women! They have not the strong heart, the cruelty, the fierce imagination that go to the making of a great artist. Even among the men of the day, corrupted and distracted as they are by foreign innovations, could real strength be found? Alas! Art was surely doomed, and his own life,—the life of the last great Kano, futile and perishable as the withering flowers on their stems.

He ate of his fish and rice in gloomy silence. Umè's gentle words failed to bring a reply. When the breakfast dishes were removed the old man continued listlessly in his place, staring out with unseeing eyes into his garden.

A loud knock came to the wooden entrance gate near the kitchen. Kano heard a man's deep tones, Mata's thin voice answering an enquiry, and then the soft murmur of Umè's words. An instant later, heavy footsteps, belonging evidently to a wearer of foreign shoes, came around by the side of the house toward the garden. Kano looked up, frowning with annoyance. A fine-looking man of middle age appeared. Kano's irritation vanished.

"Ando Uchida!" he cried aloud, springing to his feet, and hurrying to the edge of the veranda. "Ando Uchida, is it indeed you? How stout and strong and prosperous you seem! Welcome!"

"A little too stout for warm weather," laughed Ando, as laboriously he removed his foreign shoes and accepted his host's assistance up the one stone step to the veranda.

"Welcome, Ando Uchida," said Kano again, when they had taken seats. "It is quite five years since my eyes last hung upon your honorable face."

"Is it indeed so long?" said the other. "Time has the wings of a dragon-fly!"

Ando had brought with him a roll, apparently of papers, tied up in yellow cloth. This parcel he put carefully behind him on the matted floor. He then drew from his kimono sleeve a pink-bordered foreign pocket-handkerchief, and began to mop his damp forehead. Kano's politeness could not hide, entirely, a shudder of antipathy. He hurried into new speech. "And where, if it is not rude to ask, has my friend Ando sojourned during the long absence?"

"Chiefly among the mountains of Kiu Shiu," answered the other.

"Kiu Shiu," murmured the artist. "I wandered there in youth and have thought always to return. The rocks and cliffs are of great beauty. I remember well one white, thin waterfall that flung itself out like a laugh, but never reached a thing so dull as earth. Midway it was splintered upon a sunbeam, and changed into rainbows, pearls, and swallows!"

"I know it excellently well," said Uchida. "Indeed I have been zealous to preserve it, chiefly for your sake."

"Preserve it? What can you mean?"

"I have become a government inspector of mines," explained Uchida, in some embarrassment. "I thought you knew. There is a rich coal deposit near that waterfall."

"Ando! Ando!" groaned the old man, "you were once an artist! The foreigners are tainting us all."

"I love art still," said Ando, "but I make a better engineer. And—I beseech you to overlook my vulgarity—I am getting rich."

Kano groaned again. "Oh, this foreign influence! It is the curse of modern Japan! Love of money is starting a dry rot in the land of the gods. Success, material power, money,—all of them illusions, miasma of the soul, blinding men to reality! Surely my karma was evil that I needed to be reborn into this age of death!"

Ando looked sympathetic and a little contrite. "Since we are indeed hopelessly of the present," ventured he, "may it not be as well to let the foreigners teach us their methods of success?"

"Success?" cried Kano, almost angrily. "What do they succeed in except the grossest material gains? There is no humanity in them. Love of beauty dies in the womb. Shall we strive to become as dead things?"

"The love of beauty will never perish in this land," said Ando more earnestly than he had yet spoken. "A Japanese loves Art as he loves life. Our rich merchants become the best patrons of the artists."

"Patrons of the artists," echoed Kano, wearily. "You voice your own degradation, friend Ando. In the great days, who dared to speak of patronage to us. Emperors were artists and artists Emperors! It was to us that all men bowed."

"Yes, yes, that is honorably true," Ando hastened to admit. "And so would they in this age bow to you, if you would but allow it."

"I am not worthy of homage," said Kano, his head falling forward on his breast. "None knows this better than I,—and yet I am the greatest among them. Show me one of our young artists who can stand like Fudo in the flame of his own creative thought! There is none!"

"What you say is unfortunately true of the present Tokyo painters,—perhaps equally of Kioto and other large cities,—but——" Here Ando paused as if to arouse expectancy. Kano did not look up. "But," insisted the other, "may it not be possible that in some place far from the clamor of modern progress,—in some remote mountain pass,—maybe——"

Kano looked up now sharply enough. Apathy and indifference flared up like straws in a sudden flame of passion. He made a fierce gesture. "Not that, not that!" he cried. "I cannot bear it! Do not seek to give false life to a hope already dead. I am an old man. I have hoped and prayed too long. I must go down to my grave without an heir,—even an adopted heir,—for there is no disciple worthy to succeed!"

"Dear friend, believe that I would not willingly add to a grief like this. I assure you——" Ando was beginning, when his words were cut short by the entrance of Umè-ko. She bore a tray with cups, a tiny steaming tea-pot, and a dish heaped with cakes in the forms and tints of morning-glories. This offering she placed near Uchida; and then, retiring a few steps, bowed to the floor, drawing her breath inaudibly as a token of welcome and respect. Being merely a woman, old Kano did not think of presenting her. She left the room noiselessly as she had come. Ando watched every movement with admiration and a certain weighing of possibilities in his shrewd face. He nodded as if to himself, and leaned toward Kano.

"Was that not Kano Umè-ko, your daughter?"

"Yes," said the old man, gruffly; "but she is not a son."

"Fortunately for the eyes of men she is not," smiled Ando. "That is the most beautiful woman I have ever seen, and I have seen many. She welcomed me at the gate."

Kano, engaged in pouring tea, made no reply.

"Also, if current speech be true, she has great talent," persisted the visitor. "One can see genius burning like a soft light behind her face. I hear everywhere of her beauty and her fame."

"Oh, she does well,—even remarkably well for a woman," admitted Kano. "But, as I said before, she is a woman, and nothing alters that. I tell you, Ando!" he cried, in a small new gust of irritation, "sometimes I have wished that she had been left utterly untouched by art. She paints well now, because my influence is never lifted. She knows nothing else. I have allowed no lover to approach. Yet, some day love will find her, as one finds a blossoming plum tree in the night. In every rock and tree she paints I can see the hint of that coming lover; in her flowers, exquisitely drawn, nestle the faces of her children. She knows it not, but I know,—I know! She thinks she cares only for her father and her art. When I die she will marry, and then how many pictures will she paint? Bah!"

"Poor child!" murmured Ando, under his breath.

"Poor child," mocked the artist, whose quick ears had caught the whisper. "Poor Nippon, rather, and poor old Kano, who has no better heir than this frail girl. Oh, Ando, I have clamored to the gods! I have made pilgrimages and given gifts,—but there is no one to inherit my name and the traditions of my race. Nowhere can I find a Dragon Painter!"

Ando put his hand out quickly behind him, seized the long roll tied in yellow cloth, and began to unfasten it.

Kano was panting with the vehemence of his own speech. He poured another little cup of tea and drained it. He began now to watch Ando, and found himself annoyed by the deliberation of his friend's motions. "Strange, strange——" Ando was murmuring. An instant later came the whisper, "very, very strange!"

"Why do you repeat it?" cried Kano, irritably. "There was nothing strange in what I said."

The parcel was now untied. Ando held a roll of papers outward. "Examine these, Kano Indara," he said impressively. "If I do not greatly mistake, the gods, at last, have heard your prayer."

Kano went backward as if from fire. "No! I cannot,—I must not hope! Too long have I searched. Not a schoolboy who thought he could draw an outline in the sand with his toe but I have fawned on him. I dare not look. Ando, to-day I am shaken as if with an ague of the soul. I—I—could not bear another disappointment." He did indeed seem piteously weak and old. He hid his face in long, lean, twitching fingers.

Ando was sincerely affected. "This is to be no disappointment," said he, gently. "I pray you, listen patiently to my clumsy speech."

"I will strive to listen calmly," said Kano, in a broken voice. "But first honorably secrete the papers once again. They tantalize my sight."

Uchida put them down on the floor beside him and threw the cloth carelessly above. He was more moved than he cared to show. He strove now to speak simply, directly, and with convincing earnestness. Kano had settled into his old attitude of dejection.

"One morning, not more than six weeks ago," began Uchida, "the engineering party which I command had climbed some splintered peaks of the Kiu Shiu range to a spot quite close, indeed, to that thin waterfall which you remember——"

"One might forget his friends and relatives, but not a waterfall like that!" interrupted Kano.

"Suddenly a storm, blown down apparently from a clear sky, caught up the mountain and our little group of men in a great blackness."

"The mountain deities were angered at your presumption," nodded Kano, well pleased.

"It may be," admitted the other. "At any rate, the winds now hurried in from the sea. Round cloud vapors split sidewise on the wedges of the rocks. Voices screamed in the fissures. We clung to the scrub-pines and the sa-sa grass for safety."

"I can see it all. I can feel it," whispered old Kano.

"We wished to descend, but knew no way. I shouted for aid. The others shouted many times. Then from the very midst of tumult came a youth,—half god, half beast, with wild eyes peering at us, and hair that tossed like the angry clouds."

"Yes, yes," urged Kano, straining forward.

"We scrambled toward him, and he shrank back into the mist. We called, beseeching help. The workmen thought him a young sennin, and falling on their knees, began to pray. Then the youth approached us more deliberately, and, when we asked for guidance, led us by a secluded path down into a mountain village."

"And you think,—you think that this marvellous youth," began Kano, eagerly; then broke off with a gesture of despair. "I must not believe, I must not believe," he muttered.

Ando's hand was once more on the roll of papers. He went on smoothly. "We questioned of him in the village. He is a foundling. None knows his parentage. From childhood he has made pictures upon rocks, and sand beds, and the inner bark of trees. He wanders for days together among the peaks, and declares that he is searching for his mate, a Dragon Princess, withheld from him by enchantment. Naturally the village people think him mad. But they are kind to him. They give him food and clothing, and sometimes sheets of paper, like these here." With affected unconcern he raised the long roll. "Yes, they give him paper, with real ink and brushes. Then he leaps up the mountain side and paints and paints for hours, like a demon. But as soon as he has eased his soul of a sketch he lets the first gust of wind blow it away."

Kano was now shivering in his place. On his wrinkled face a light dawned. "Shall I believe? Oh, Ando, indeed I could not bear it now! Unroll those drawings before I go mad!"

Uchida deliberately spread out the first. It was a scene of mountain storm, painted as in an elemental fury. Inky pine branches slashed and hurled upward, downward, and across a tortured gray sky. A cloud-rack tore the void like a Valkyrie's cry made visible. One huge talon of lightning clutched at the flying scud.

Kano gave a glance, covered his face, and began to sob. Uchida blew his nose on the pink-bordered foreign handkerchief. After a long while the old man whispered, "What name shall I use in my prayer?"

"He is called," said Ando, "by the name of 'Tatsu.' 'Tatsu, the Dragon Painter.'"

II

The sounds and sights of the great capital were dear to Ando Uchida. In five years of busy exile among remote mountains he felt that he had earned, as it were, indulgence for an interval of leisurely enjoyment.

His initial visit to old Kano had been made not so much to renew an illustrious acquaintance, as to relieve his own mind of its exciting news, and his hands of a parcel which, at every stage of the journey, had been an incubus. Ando knew the paintings to be unusual. He had hoped for and received from Kano the highest confirmation of this belief.

At that time, now a week ago, he had been pleased, and Kano irradiated. Already he was cursing himself for his pains, and crying aloud that, had he dreamed the consequences, never had the name of Tatsu crossed his lips! Ando's anticipated joys in Yeddo lay, as yet, before him. Hourly was he tormented by visits from the impatient Kano. Neither midnight nor dawn were safe from intrusion. Always the same questions were asked, the same fears spoken, the same glorious future prophesied; until finally, in despair, one night Ando arose between the hours of two and three, betaking himself to a small suburban hotel. Here he lived, for a time, in peace, under the protection of an assumed name.

A letter had been dispatched that first day, to Tatsu of Kiu Shiu, with a sum of money for the defraying of travelling expenses, and the petition that the youth should come as quickly as possible for a visit to Kano Indara, since the old man could not, of himself, attempt so long a journey. After what seemed to the impatient writer (and in equal degree to the harassed Uchida) an endless cycle of existence, an answer came, not, indeed from Tatsu, but from the "Mura osa," or head of the village, saying that the Mad Painter had started at once upon his journey, taking not even a change of clothes. By what route he would travel or on what date arrive, only the gods could tell.

Kano's rapture in these tidings was assailed, at once, by a swarm of black conjectures. Might the boy not lose himself by the way? If he attempted to ride upon the hideous foreign trains he was certain to be injured; if on the other hand, he did not come by train, weeks, even months, might be consumed in the journey. Again, should he essay to come by boat! Then there were dangers of wind and storm. Visions of Tatsu drowned; of Tatsu heaped under a wreck of burning cars; starved to death in a solitary forest; set upon, robbed, and slain by footpads, all spun—black silhouettes in a revolving lantern—through Kano's frenzied imagination. It was at this point that Uchida had hid himself, and assumed a false name.

In another week the gentle Umè began to grow pale and silent under the small tyrannies of her father. Mata openly declared her belief that it was a demon now on the way to them, since he had power to change the place into a cave of torment even before arrival. After Uchida's defection old Kano remained constantly at home. Many hours at a time he stood upon the moon-viewing hillock of his garden, staring up, then down the street, up and down, up and down, until it was weariness to watch him. Within the rooms he was merely one curved ear, bent in the direction of the entrance gate. His nervousness communicated itself to the women of the house. They, too, were listening. More than one innocent visitor had been thrown into panic by the sight of three strained faces at the gate, and three pairs of shining eyes set instantly upon them.

One twilight hour, late in August, Tatsu came. After an eager day of watching, old Kano had just begun to tell himself that hope was over. Tatsu had certainly been killed. The ihai might as well be set up, and prayers offered for the dead man's soul. Umè-ko, wearied by the heat, and the incessant strain, lay prone upon her matted floor, listening to the chirp of a bell cricket that hung in a tiny bamboo cage near by. The clear notes of the refrain, struck regularly with the sound of a fairy bell, had begun to help and soothe her. Mata sat dozing on the kitchen step.

A loud, sudden knock shattered in an instant this precarious calm. Kano went through the house like a storm. Mata, being nearest, flung the panel of the gate aside. There stood a creature with tattered blue robe just to the knees, bare feet, bare head, with wild, tossing locks of hair, and eyes that gleamed with a panther's light.

"Is it—is it—Tatsu?" screamed the old man, hurling his voice before him.

"It is a madman," declared the servant, and flattened herself against the hedge.

Umè said nothing at all. After one look into the stranger's face she had withdrawn, herself unseen, into the shadowy rooms.

"I am Tatsu of Kiu Shiu," announced the apparition, in a voice of strange depth and sweetness. "Is this the home of Kano Indara?"

"Yes, yes, I am Kano Indara," said the artist, almost grovelling on the stones. "Enter, dear sir, I beseech. You must be weary. Accompany me in this direction, august youth. Mata, bring tea to the guest-room."

Tatsu followed his tempestuous host in silence. As they gained the room Kano motioned him to a cushion, and prepared to take a seat opposite. Tatsu suddenly sank to his knees, bowing again and again, stiffly, in a manner long forgotten in fashionable Yeddo.

"Discard the ceremony of bowing, I entreat," said Kano.

"Why? Is it not a custom here?"

"Yes,—to a lesser extent. But between us, dear youth, it is unnecessary."

"Why should it be unnecessary between us?" persisted the unsmiling guest.

"Because we are artists, therefore brothers," explained Kano, in an encouraging voice.

Tatsu frowned. "Who are you, and why have you sent for me?"

"Do you inquire who I am?" said Kano, scarcely believing his ears.

"It is what I asked."

"I am Kano Indara." The old man folded his arms proudly, waiting for the effect.

Tatsu moved impatiently upon his velvet cushion. "Of course I knew that. It was the name on the scrap of paper that guided me here."

"Is it possible that you do not yet know the meaning of the name of Kano?" asked the artist, incredulously. A thin red tingled to his cheek,—the hurt of childish vanity.

"There is one of that name in my village," said Tatsu. "He is a scavenger, and often gives me fine large sheets of paper."

Old Kano's lip trembled. "I am not of his sort. Men call me an artist."

"Oh, an artist! Does that mean a painter of dragons, like me?"

"Among other things of earth and air I have attempted to paint dragons," said Kano.

"I paint nothing else," declared Tatsu, and seemed to lose interest in the conversation.

Kano looked hard into his face. "You say that you paint nothing else?" he challenged. "Are not these—all of them—your work, the creations of your fancy?" He reached out for the roll that Uchida had brought. His hands trembled. In his nervous excitement the papers fell, scattering broadcast over the floor.

Tatsu's dark face flashed into light. "My pictures! My pictures!" he cried aloud, like a child. "They always blow off down the mountain!"

Kano picked up a study at random. It was of a mountain tarn lying quiet in the sun. Trees in a windless silence sprang straight upward from the brink. Beyond and above these a few tall peaks stood thin and pale, cutting a sky that was empty of all but light.

"Where is the dragon here?" challenged the old man.

"Asleep under the lake."

"And where here?" he asked quickly, in order to hide his discomfiture. The second picture was a scene of heavy rain descending upon a village. "Oh, I perceive for myself," he hurried on before Tatsu could reply. "The dragon lies full length, half sleeping, on the soaking cloud."

Tatsu's lip curled, but he remained silent.

The old man's hands rattled among the edges of the papers. "Ah, here, Master Painter, are you overthrown!" he cried triumphantly, lifting the painting of a tall girl who swayed against a cloudy background. The lines of the thin gray robe blew lightly to one side. The whole figure had the poise and lightness of a vision; yet in the face an exquisite human tenderness smiled out. "Show me a dragon here," repeated Kano.

Tatsu looked troubled and, for the first time, studied intently the countenance of his host. "Surely, honored sir, if you are a painter, as you say you are, its meaning must be plain. Look more closely. Do you not see on what the maiden stands?"

"Of course I see," snapped Kano. "She stands among rocks and weeds, and looks marvellously like——" He broke off, thinking it better not to mention his daughter's name. "But I repeat, no dragon-thought is here."

Tatsu reached out, took the picture, and tore it into shreds. Then he rose to his feet. "Good-by," he said. "I shall now make a quick returning. You are of the blind among men. My painting was the Dragon Maid, standing on the peaks of earth. All my life I have sought her. The people of my village think me mad because of her. By reason that I cannot find, I paint. Good-by!"

"Good-by!" echoed the other. "What do you mean? What are you saying?" The face of a horrible possibility jeered at him. His heart pounded the lean ribs and stood still. Tatsu was upon his feet. In an instant more he would be gone forever.

"Tatsu, wait!" almost screamed the old man. "Surely you cannot mean to return when you have but now arrived! Be seated. I insist! There is much to talk about."

"I have nothing to talk about. When a thing is to be done, then it is best to do it quickly. Good-by!" He wheeled toward the deepening night, the torn and soiled blue robe clinging to him as to the figure of a primeval god.

"Tatsu! Tatsu!" cried the other in an agony of fear. "Stop! I command!"

Tatsu turned, scowling. Then he laughed.

"No, no, I did not mean the word 'command.' I entreat you, Tatsu, because you are young and I am old; because I need you. Dear youth, you must be hungered and very weary. Remain at least until our meal is served."

"I desire no food of yours," said Tatsu. "Why did you summon me when you had nothing to reveal? You are no artist! And I pine, already, for the mountains!"

"Then, Tatsu, if I am no artist, stay and teach me how to paint. Yes, yes, you shall honorably teach me. I shall receive reproof thankfully. I need you, Tatsu. I have no son. Stay and be my son."

The short, scornful laugh came again. "Your son! What could you do with a son like me? You love to dwell in square cages, and wear smooth shiny clothes. You eat tasteless foods and sleep like a cocoon that is rolled. My life is upon the mountains; my food the wild grapes and the berries that grow upon them. The pheasants and the mountain lions are my friends. I stifle in these lowlands. I cannot stay. I must breathe the mountains, and there among the peaks some day—some day—I shall touch her sleeve, the sleeve of the Dragon Maiden whom I seek. Let me go, old man! I have no business in this place!"

In extremes of desperation one clutches at the semblance of a straw. A last, wild hope had flashed to Kano's mind. "Come nearer, Tatsu San," he whispered, forcing his face into the distortion of a smile. "Lean nearer. The real motive of my summons has not been spoken."

Compelled by the strange look and manner of his host, Tatsu retraced a few steps. The old voice wheedled through the dusk. "In this very house, under my mortal control, the Dragon Maiden whom you seek is hidden."

Tatsu staggered back, then threw himself to the floor, searching the speaker's face for truth. "Could you lie to me of such a thing as this?" he asked.

"No, Tatsu, by the spirits of my ancestors, I have such a maiden here. Soon I shall show you. Only you must be patient and very quiet, that she may manifest herself."

"I shall be quiet, Kano Indara."

Kano, shivering now with excitement and relief, clapped hands loudly and called on Mata's name. The old dame entered, skirting warily the vicinity of the "madman."

"Mata, fix your eyes on me only while I am speaking," began her master. "Say to the Dragon Maid whom we keep in the chamber by the great plum tree that I, Kano Indara, command her to appear. The costume must be worn; and let her enter, singing. These are my instructions. Assist the maiden to obey them. Go!"

His piercing look froze the questions on her tongue. "And Mata," he called again, stopping her at the threshold, "bring at once some heated sakè,—the best,—and follow it closely with the evening meal."

"Kashikomarimashita," murmured the servant, dutifully. But within the safety of her kitchen she exploded into execrations, muttering prophecies of evil, with lamentations that a Mad Thing from the mountains had broken into the serenity of their lives.

Tatsu, who had listened eagerly to the commands, now flung back his head and drew a long breath. "My life being spent among wild creatures," he murmured as if to himself, "little skill have I in judging the ways of men. How shall I believe that in this desert of houses a true Dragon Maiden can be found?" Again he turned flashing eyes upon his host. "I mistrust you, Kano Indara! Your thin face peers like a fox from its hole. If you deceive me,—yet must I remain,—for should she come———"

"You shall soon perceive for yourself, dear Dragon Youth."

Mata entered with hot sakè. "Go! We shall serve ourselves," said Kano, much to her relief.

"I seldom drink," observed Tatsu, as the old man filled his cup. "Once it made of me a fool. But I will take a little now, for I am very weary with the long day."

"Indeed, it must be so; but good wine refreshes the body and the mind alike," replied the other. It was hard to pour the sakè with such shaking hands, harder still to keep his eyes from the beautiful sullen face so near him, and yet he forced the wrinkled eyelids to conceal his dawning joy. In Tatsu's strange submission, the artist felt that the new glory of the Kano name was being born.

III

For a long interval the two men sat in silence. Kano leaned forward from time to time, filling the small cup which Tatsu—half in revery it seemed—had once more drained. The old servant now and again crept in on soundless feet to replace with a freshly heated bottle of sakè the one grown cold. So still was the place that the caged cricket hanging from the eaves of Umè's distant room beat time like an elfin metronome.

Two of the four walls of the guest-room were of shoji, a lattice covered with translucent rice-paper. These opened directly upon the garden. The third wall, a solid one of smoke-blue plaster, held the niche called "tokonoma," where pictures are hung and flower vases set. The remaining wall, opening toward the suite of chambers, was fashioned of four great sliding doors called fusuma, dull silver of background, with paintings of shadowy mountain landscape done centuries before by one of the greatest of the Kanos. It was in front of these doors that Mata now placed two lighted candles in tall bronze holders.

Outside, the garden became a blur of soft darkness. Within, the flickering yellow light of the candles danced through the room, touching now the old face, now the young, each set hard in its own lines of concentrated thought. Weird shadows played about the mountains on the silver doors, and hid in far corners of the matted floor.

All at once the two central fusuma were apart. No slightest sound had been made, yet there, in the narrow rectangle, stood a figure,—surely not of earth,—a slim form in misty gray robes, wearing a crown of intertwisted dragons, with long filigree chains that fell straight to the shoulders. In one hand was held an opened fan of silver.

Tatsu gave a convulsive start, then checked himself. He could not believe the vision real. Not even in his despairing dreams had the Dragon Maid appeared so exquisite. As he gazed, one white-clad foot slid a few inches toward him on the shining floor. Another step, and she was in the room. The fusuma behind her closed as noiselessly as they had opened. Tatsu shivered a little, and stared on. With equal intensity the old man watched the face of Tatsu.

The figure had begun to sway, slightly, at full length, like long bands of perpendicular rain across the face of a mountain. A singing voice began, rich, passionate, and low, matching with varying intonation the marvellous postures of fan and throat and body. At first low in sound, almost husky, it flowered to a note long held and gradually deepening in power. It gathered up shadows from the heart and turned them into light.

Umè-ko danced (or so she would have told you) only to fulfil her father's command; yet, before she had reached the room, she knew that it would be such a dance as neither she nor the old artist had dreamed of. That first glimpse of Tatsu's face at the gate had registered for her a notch upon the Revolving Wheel of Life. His first spoken word had aroused in her strange mystic memories from stranger hiding places. Karma entered with her into the little guest-room where she was to dance and charged the very air with revelation. The words of the old classic poem she had in her ignorance believed familiar, she knew that she was now for the first time really to sing.

"Not for one life but for the blossoming of a thousand lives, shall I seek my lover, shall I regain his love," she sang. No longer was it Umè-ko at all, but in actual truth the Dragon Maid, held from her lover by a jealous god, seeking him through fire and storm and sea, peering for him into the courts of emperors, the shrines of the astonished gods, the very portals of the under-world.

And Tatsu listened without sound or motion; only his eyes burned like beacons in a windless night. Kano wriggled himself backward on the matting that the triumph of his face might not be seen. Now and again he leaned forward stealthily and filled Tatsu's cup.

The unaccustomed fluid was already pouring in a fiery torrent through the boy's vivid brain. His hands, slipped within the tattered blue sleeves, grasped tightly each the elbow of the other arm. His ecstacy was a drug, enveloping his senses; again it was a fire that threatened the very altar of his soul. Through it all he, as Umè-ko, realized fulfilment. Here in this desert of men's huts he had gained what all the towering mountains had not been able to bestow. Here was his bride, made manifest, his mate, the Dragon Maid, found at last through centuries of barren searching! Surely, if he should spring now to his feet, catch her to him and call upon his mountain gods for aid, they would be hurled together to some paradise of love where only he and she and love would be alive! He trembled and caught in his breath with a sob. Kano glided a few feet nearer, and struck the matting sharply with his hand.

Suddenly the dance was over. Umè-ko, quivering now in every limb, sank to the floor. She bowed first to the guest of honor, then to her father. Touching her wet eyes with a silken sleeve she moved backward to the rear of the room where she seated herself upright, motionless as the wall itself, between the two tall candles. Tatsu's eyes never left her face. Old Kano, in the background, rocked to and fro, and, after a short pause of waiting, clapped his hands for Mata.

"Hai-ie-ie-ie-ie!" came the thin voice, long drawn out, from the kitchen. She entered with a tray of steaming food, placing it before Tatsu. A second tray was brought for the master, and a fresh bottle of wine. Umè-ko sat motionless against the silver fusuma, an ivory image, crowned and robed in shimmering gray.

The odor of good food attracted Tatsu's senses if not his eyes. He ate greedily, hastily, not seeing what he ate. His manners were those of an untutored mountain peasant.

"Dragon Maid," purred Kano, "weariness has come upon you. Retire, I pray, and deign to rest."

"No!" said Tatsu, loudly. "She shall not leave this room."

"My concern is for the august maiden who has found favor in your sight," replied Kano, with a deprecating gesture. "Here, Tatsu, let me fill your cup."

Tatsu threw his cup face down to the floor, and put his lean, brown hand upon it. "I drink no more until my cup of troth with the maiden yonder."

Umè-ko's startled eyes flew to his. She trembled, and the blood slowly ebbed from her face, leaving it pale and luminous with a sort of wonder.

"Go!" said Kano again, and, in a daze, the girl rose and vanished from the room.

Tatsu had hurled himself toward her, but it was too late. He turned angrily to his host. "She is mine! Why did you send her away?"

"Gently, gently," cooed the other. "In this incarnation she is called my daughter."

"I believe it not!" cried Tatsu. "How came she under bondage to you? Have I not sought her through a thousand lives? She is mine!"

"Even so, in this life I am her father, and it is my command that she will obey."

Tatsu rocked and writhed in his place.

"She is a good daughter," pursued the other, amiably. "She has never yet failed in docility and respect. Without my consent you shall not touch her,—not even her sleeve."

"I have sought her through a thousand lives. I will slay him who tries to keep her from me!" raved the boy.

"To kill her father would scarcely be a fortunate beginning," said Kano, tranquilly. "Your hope lies in safer paths, dear youth. There are certain social conventions attached even to a Dragon Maid. Now if you will calm yourself and listen to reason——"

Tatsu sprang to his feet and struck himself violently upon the brow. The hot wine was making a whirlpool of his brain. "Reason! convention! safety! I hate them all! Oh, you little men of cities! Farmyard fowls and swine, running always to one sty, following always one lead,—doing things in the one way that other base creatures have marked out——"

Kano laughed aloud. His whole life had been a protest against conventionality, and this impassioned denunciation came from a new world. The sound maddened Tatsu. He leaped to the veranda, now a mere ledge thrust out over darkness, threw an arm about the slender corner-post, and strained far out, gasping, into the night. Kano filled his pipe with leisurely deliberation. The time was past for fear.

In a few moments the boy returned, his face ugly, black, and sullen. "I will be your son if you give me the maiden," he muttered.

"Come now, this is much better," said Kano, with a genial smile. "We shall discuss the matter like rational men."

Tatsu ground his teeth so that the other heard him.

"Have a pipe," said Kano.

"I want no pipe."

"At least make yourself at ease upon the cushion while I speak."

"I am more at ease without it," said the boy, flinging the velvet square angrily across the room. "Ugh! It is like sitting on a dead cat. Kindly speak without further care for me. I am at ease!"

Kano glanced at the burning eyes, the quivering face and twitching muscles with a smile. The intensity of ardor touched him. He drew a short sigh, the look of complacency left his for an instant, and he began, deliberately, "As you may have gathered from my letter, I am without a son."

Tatsu nodded shortly.

"Worse than this, among all my disciples here in Yeddo there has appeared none worthy to inherit the name and traditions of my race. Now, dear youth, when I first saw these paintings of yours, the hope stirred in me that you might be that one."

"Do you mean that I should paint things as paltry as your own?"

"No, not exactly, though even from my poor work you might gain some valuable lessons of technique."

"I know not that word," said Tatsu. "When I must paint, I paint. What has all this to do with the Dragon Maiden?"

"Softly, softly; we are coming to that now," said Kano. "If, after trial, I should find you really worthy of adoption, nothing could be more appropriate than for you to become the husband of my daughter."

Tatsu dug his nails into the matting of the floor. "Suitable—appropriate—husband!" he groaned aloud. "Farmyard cackle,—all of it. Oh, to be joined in the manner of such earthlings to a Dragon Maid like this! Old man, cannot even you feel the horror of it? No, your eyes blink like a pig that has eaten. You cannot see. She should be made mine among storm and wind and mist on some high mountain peak, where the gods would lean to us, and great straining forests roar out our marriage hymn!"

"There is indeed something about it that appeals to me. It would make a fine subject for a painting."

"Oh, oh," gasped Tatsu, and clutched at his throat. "When will you give her to me, Kano Indara? Shall it be to-night?"

"To-night? Are you raving!" cried the astonished Kano. "It would be at the very least a month."

Tatsu rose and staggered to the veranda. "A month!" he whispered to the stars. "Shall I live at all? Good-night, old man of clay," he called suddenly, and with a light step was down upon the garden path.

Kano hurried to him. "Stop, stop, young sir," he called half clicked, now, with laughter. "Do not go in this rude way. You are my guest. The women are even now preparing your bed."

"I lie not on beds," jeered Tatsu through the darkness. "Vile things they are, like the ooze that smears the bottom of a lake. I climb this hillside for my couch. To-morrow, with the sun, I shall return!"

The voice, trailing away through silence and the night, had a tone of supernatural sweetness. When it had quite faded Kano stared on, for a long time, into the fragrant solitude. Stars were out now by thousands, a gold mosaic set into a high purple dome. Off to the south a wide blur of artificial light hung above the city, the visible expression, as it were, of the low, human roar of life, audible even in this sheltered nook. To the north, almost it seemed within touch of his hands, the temple cliff rose black, formidable, and impressive, a gigantic wall of silence. The camphor tree overhead was thrown out darkly against the stars, like its own shadow. The velvety boom of the temple bell, striking nine, held in its echoes the color and the softness of the hour.

Kano, turning at last from the veranda, slowly re-entered the guest-room, and seated himself upon one of the cushions that had aroused Tatsu's scorn. A dead cat,—forsooth! Well to old bones a dead cat might be better than no cushion! Mata had come in very softly. "I prayed the gods for him," Kano was muttering aloud, "and I thank them that he is here. To-morrow I shall make offering at the temple. Yet I have thanks, too, that there is but one of him. Ah, Mata,—you? My hot bath, is it ready? And, friend Mata, do you recall a soothing draught you once prepared for me at a time of great mental strain,—there was, I think, something I wished to do with a picture, and the picture would not allow it. I should like a draught like that to-night."

"Kashikomarimashita. I recall it," said old Mata, grimly, "and I shall make it strong, for you have something worse than pictures to deal with now."

"Thanks. I was sure you would remember," smiled the old man, and Mata, disarmed of her cynicism, could say no more.

Umè remained in her chamber. She had not been seen since the dance. All her fusuma and shoji were closed. Mata, in leaving her master, looked tentatively toward this room, but after an imperceptible pause kept on down the central passageway of the house to the bathroom, at the far end. The place smelled of steam, of charcoal fumes, and cedar wood. With two long, thin iron "fire-sticks," Mata poked, from the top, the heap of darkening coals in the cylindrical furnace that was built into one end of the tub. For the protection of the bather this was surrounded with a wooden lattice which, being always wet when the furnace was in use, never charred. The tub itself was of sugi-wood. After years of service it still gave out unfailingly its aromatic breath, and felt soft to the touch, like young leaves. Sighing heavily, the old servant bared her arm and leaned over to stir the water, to draw down by long, elliptical swirls of motion the heated upper layers into cold strata at the bottom. She then wiped her arm on her apron and went to the threshold of the guest-room to inform the waiting occupant. "In ten minutes more, without fail, the water will be at right heat for your augustness."

Now, in the kitchen, a great searching among jars and boxes on high shelves told of preparation for the occasional brew. Again she thought of calling Umè. Umè could reach the highest shelf without standing on an inverted rice-pot, or the even more precarious fish-cleaning bench. And again, for a reason not quite plain to herself, Mata decided not to call. She threw a fresh handful of twigs and dried ferns to the sleeping ashes of the brazier, set a copper skillet deep into the answering flame, and began dropping dried bits of herbs into the simmering water. Instantly the air was changed,—was tinged and interpenetrated with hurrying, spicy fumes, with hints of a bitter bark, of jellied gums, of resin, and a compelling odor which should have been sweet, but was only nauseating. The steam assumed new colors as it rose. Each sprite of aromatic perfume when released plunged into noiseless tumult with opposing fumes. The kitchen was a crucible, and the old dame a mediaeval alchemist. The flames and smoke striving upward, as if to reach her bending face, made it glow with the hue of the copper kettle, a wrinkled copper, etched deep with lines of life, of merriment, perplexity, of shrewd and practical experience.

As she stirred, testing by nose and eye the rapid completion of her work, she was determining to put aside for her own use a goodly share of the beneficent fluid. The coming of the wild man had unnerved her terribly. In the threatening family change she could perceive nothing but menace. Apprehension even now weighed down upon her, a foreshadowing of evil that had, somehow, a present hostage in the deep silence of Umè's room. Of what was her nursling thinking? How had it seemed to her, so guarded, and so delicately reared, this being summoned like a hired geisha to dance before a stranger,—a ragged, unkempt, hungry stranger! Even her father's well-known madness for things of art could scarcely atone to his child for this indignity.

Kano had gone promptly to his bath. He was now emerging. His bare feet grazed the wooden corridor. Mata ran to him. "Good! Ah, that was good!" he said heartily. "Five years of aches have I left in the tub!" Within his chamber the andon was already lighted, and the long, silken bed-cushions spread. Mata assisted him to slip down carefully between the mattress and the thin coverlid. She patted and arranged him as she would a child, and then went to fetch the draught. "Mata, thou art a treasure," he said, as she knelt beside him, the bowl outstretched. He drained the last drop, and the old friends exchanged smiles of answering satisfaction. Before leaving him she trimmed and lowered the andon so that its yellow light would be a mere glimmer in the darkness.

She moved now deliberately to Umè's fusuma, tapping lightly on the lacquered frame. "Miss Umè! O Jo San!" she called. Nothing answered.

Mata parted the fusuma an inch. The Japanese matted floor, even in darkness, gives out a sort of ghostly, phosphorescent glow. Thus, in the unlit space Mata could perceive that the girl lay at full length, her Dragon Robe changed to an ordinary house dress, her long hair unbound, her face turned downward and hidden on an outstretched arm. It was not a pose of grief, neither did it hint of slumber.

"Honorable Young Lady of the House," said Mata, now more severely, "I came to announce your bath. The august father having already entered and withdrawn, it is your turn."

This time Umè answered her, not, however, changing her position. "I do not care to take the bath to-night. You enter, I pray, without further waiting. I—I—should like to be left alone, nurse. I myself will unroll the bed and light the andon."

Mata leaned nearer. Her voice was a theatrical whisper. "Is it that you are outraged, my Umè-ko, at your father's strange demand upon you? I was myself angered. He would scarcely have done so much for a Prince of the Blood,—and to make you appear before so crude and ignorant a thing as that—"

Umè sat upright. "No, I am angered at nothing. I only wish to be alone. Ah, nurse, you have always spoiled me,—give me my way."

Mata went off grumbling. She wished that Umè had shown a more natural indignation. The hot bath, however, notwithstanding Kano's five lost years of pain presumably in solution, brought her ease of body, as did the soothing potion, ease of mind.

All night long the old folks heavily slept; and all night long little Umè-ko drifted in a soft, slow rising flood of consciousness that was neither sleep nor waking, though wrought of the intertwining strands of each. Again she saw the dark face in the gateway. It was a mere picture in a frame, set for an artist's joy. Then it seemed a summons, calling her to unfamiliar paths,—a prophecy, a clew. Again she heard his voice,—an echo made of all these things, and more. She tried to force herself to think of him merely as an artist would think; how the lines of the shoulders and the throat flowed upward, like dark flame, to the altar of his face. How the hair grew in flame upon his brow, how the dark eyes, fearless and innocent with the look of primeval youth, indeed, held a strange human pain of searching. The mere remembered pictures of him rose and fell with her as sea-flowers, or long river grass; but when there came remembered shiver of his words, "I drink no more until my cup of troth with the maiden yonder!" then all drifting ceased; illusion was at an end. With a gasp she felt herself falling straight down through a swirling vortex of sensation, to the very sand-bed of the stream. Now she was sitting upright (the sand-bed had suddenly become the floor of her little room), her hands pressing a heart that was trying to escape, her young eyes straining through the darkness to see,—ah!—she could see nothing at all for the shining!

She listened now with bated breath, thinking that by some unconscious cry she might have aroused the others. No, Kano breathed on softly, regularly, in the next room; while from the kitchen wing came unfaltering the beat of Mata's nasal metronome.

In one such startled interval of waking her caged cricket had given out its plaintive cry. All at once it seemed to Umè-ko an unbearable thing for any spark of life to be so prisoned. She longed to set him free, but even though she opened wide her shoji, the outer night-doors, the amado stretched, a relentless opaque wall, along the four sides of the house.

She lay quiet now for a long time. "I will return with the sun," he had said. She wished that the cricket were indeed outside, and could tell her of the first dawn-stirring. It was very close and dark in the little room. She had not lighted the andon after all. It could not be so dark outside. With very cautious fingers she began now to separate the shoji that opened on the garden side. A breath of exquisite night air rushed in to her from the lattices above the amado. It would be a difficult matter to push even one of these aside without waking the house. Yet, there were two things in her favor; the unusually heavy sleep of her companions and the fact that the amado had a starting point in their long grooves from a shallow closet very near her room. So instead of having to remove the whole chain, each clasping by a metal hand, its neighbor, she had but to unbar the initial panel, coax it noiselessly apart just far enough to emit a not too bulky form, and then the night would be hers.

There had been in the girl's life so little need of cunning or of strategy that her innocent adventure now brought a disturbing sense of crime. She had unlatched the first amado in safety, and had her white arms braced to push it to one side, when, suddenly she thought, "I am acting like a thief! Perhaps I am feeling like a thief! This is a terrible thing and must displease the gods." Her hands dropped limply, she must not continue with this deed. Somewhere near her feet the cricket gave out an importunate chirp. She stooped to him, feeling about for the little residence with tender, groping hands. She must give him freedom, though she dared not take it for herself. Yet it would be sweet to breathe the world for its own sake once more before he—and the sun—returned.

The amado went back as if of itself. In an instant Umè's face was among the dew-wet leaves of the plum tree. Oh, it was sweet! The night smelled of silence and the stars. She threw back her head to drink it like a liquid. She lifted the insect in its cage. By holding it high, against a star of special brightness, she could see the tiny bit of life gazing at her through its bars. She opened the door of the cage, and set it among the twigs of the plum. Then barefooted, ungirdled, with hair unbound, she stepped down upon the stone beneath the tree, and then to the garden path.

IV

The pebbles of the garden were slippery and cold under the feet that pressed them. Also they hurt a little. Umè longed to return for her straw sandals, but this freedom of the night was already far too precious for jeopardy. She caught her robe about her throat and was glad of the silken shawl of her long hair. How thickly shone the stars! It must be close upon the hour of their waning, yet how big and soft; and how companionable! She stretched her arms up to them, moving as if they drew her down the path. They were more real, indeed, than the dim and preternatural space in which she walked.

She looked slowly about upon that which should have been commonplace and found the outlines alone to be unaltered. There were the hillock, the house, the thick hedge-lines square at the corners with black bars hard as wood against the purple night; there were the winding paths and little courts of open gravel. She could have put her hand out, saying, "Here, on this point, should be the tall stone lantern; here, in this sheltered curve, a fern." Both lantern and fern would have been in place; and yet, despite these evidences of the usual, all that once made the sunlit garden space an individual spot, was, in this dim, ghostly air, transformed. The spirit of the whole had taken on weird meaning. It was as if Mata's face looked suddenly upon her with the old abbot's eyes. Fantastic possibilities crouched, ready to spring from every shadow. The low shrubs held themselves in attitudes of flight. This was a world in which she had no part. She knew herself a paradox, the violator of a mood; but the enchantment held her.

She had reached now the edge of the pond. It was a surface of polished lacquer, darker than the night, and powdered thick with the gold of reflected stars. Leaning over, she marvelled at the silhouette of her own slim figure. It did not seem to have an actual place among these frail phantasmagoria. As she stared on she noticed that the end of the pond farthest from her, to the west, quivered and turned gray. She looked quickly upward and around. Yes, there to the east was the answering blur of light. Dawn had begun.

She ran now to the top of the moon-viewing hill. The earth was wider here; the dawn more at home. Below her where the city used to be was no city, only a white fog-sea, without an island. The cliff, black at the base, rising gradually into thinner gray, drove through the air like the edge of a coming world. A chill breeze swept out from the hollow, breathing of waking grasses and of dew. The girl shivered, but it was with ecstacy. "I climb this hillside for my couch, to-night!" Was he too waking, watching, feeling himself intruder upon a soundless ritual? There was a hissing noise as of a fawn hurrying down a tangled slope. The hedge near the cliff end of the garden dipped and squeaked and shook indignant plumes after a figure that had desecrated its green guardianship, and was now striding ruthlessly across the enclosure.

Umè heard and saw; then wrung her hands in terror. It was he, of course,—the Dragon Painter; and he would speak with her. What could she do? Family honor must be maintained, and so she could not cry for help. Why had her heart tormented her to go into the night? Why had she not thought of this possibility? Because of it, life, happiness, everything might be wrecked, even before they had dared to think of happiness by name!

Tatsu had reached her. Leaning close he set his eyes to her face as one who drinks deep and silently.

"I must not remain. Oh, sir, let me pass!" she whispered.

He did not speak or try to touch her. A second gust of wind came from the cliff, blowing against his hand a long tress of her hair. It was warm and perfumed, and had the clinging tenderness of youth. He shivered now, as she was doing, and stood looking down at his hand. Umè made a swift motion as if to pass him; but he threw out the barrier of an arm.

"I have been calling you all the night. Now, at last, you have come. Why did you never answer me upon the mountains?"

"Indeed, I could not. I was not permitted. As you must see for yourself, lord, in this incarnation I am but a mortal maiden."

"I do not see it for myself," said Tatsu, with a low, triumphant laugh. "I see something different!" Suddenly he reached forward, caught the long ends of her hair and held them out to left and right, the full width of his arms. They stood for a moment in intense silence, gazing each into the face of the other. The rim of the dawn behind them cut, with its flat, gold disc, straight down to the heart of the world. "You a mortal!" said the boy again, exultantly. "Why, even now, your face is the white breast of a great sea-bird, your hair, its shining wings, and your soul a message that the gods have sent to me! Oh, I know you for what you are,—my Dragon Maid, my bride! Have I not sought you all these years, tracing your face on rocks and sand-beds of my hills, hanging my prayers to every blossoming tree? Come, you are mine at last; here is your master! We will escape together while the stupid old ones sleep! Come, soul of my soul, to our mountains!"

He would have seized her, but a quick, passionate gesture of repulsion kept him back. "I am the child of Kano Indara," she said. "He, too, has power of the gods, and I obey him. Oh, sir, believe that you, as I, are subject to his will, for if you set yourself against him—"

"Kano Indara concerns me not at all," cried Tatsu, half angrily. "It is with you,—with you alone, I speak!"

Umè poised at the very tip of the hill. "Look, sir,—the plum tree," she whispered, pointing. So sudden was the change in voice and manner that the other tripped and was caught by it. "That longest, leafy branch touches the very wall of my room," she went on, creeping always a little down the hill. "If you again will write such things to me, trusting your missive to that branch, I shall receive it, and—will answer. Oh, it is a bold, unheard-of thing for a girl to do, but I shall answer."

"I should like better that you meet me here each morning at this hour," said Tatsu.

The girl looked about her swiftly, gave a little cry, and clasped her hands together. "See, lord, the day comes fast. Mata, my old nurse, may already be astir. I saw a flock of sparrows fly down suddenly to the kitchen door. And there, above us, on the great camphor tree, the sun has smitten with a fist of gold!"

Tatsu gazed up, and when his eyes returned to earth he found himself companionless. He threw himself down, a miserable heap, clasping his knees upon the hill. No longer was the rosy dawn for him. He found no timid beauty in the encroaching day. His sullen look fastened itself upon the amado beneath the plum tree. The panels were now tightly closed. The house itself, soundless and gray in the fast brightening space, mocked him with impassivity.

A little later, when the neighborhood reverberated to the slamming of amado and the sharp rattle of paper dusters against taut shoji panes; when fragrant faggot smoke went up from every cottage, and the street cries of itinerant venders signalled domestic buying for the day, Mata discovered the wild man in the garden, and roused her sleeping master with the news. She went, too, to Umè's room, and was reassured to see the girl apparently in slumber within a neat bed, the andon burning temperately in its corner, and the whole place eloquent of innocence and peace, Kano shivered himself into his day clothes (the process was not long), and hurried out to meet his guest.

"O Haiyo gozaimasu!" he called. "You have found a good spot from which to view the dawn."

"Good morning!" said Tatsu, looking about as if to escape.

"Come, enter my humble house with me, young sir. Breakfast will soon be served."

Tatsu rose instantly, though the gesture was far from giving an effect of acquiescence. He shook his cramped limbs with as little ceremony as if Kano were a shrub, and then turned, with the evident intention of flight. Suddenly the instinct of hunger claimed him. Breakfast! That had a pleasant sound. And where else was he to go for food! He wheeled around to his waiting host. "I thank you. I will enter!" he said, and attempted an archaic bow.

Mata brought in to them, immediately, hot tea and a small dish of pickled plums. Kano drew a sigh of relief as he saw Tatsu take up a plum, and then accept, from the servant's hands, a cup of steaming tea. These things promised well for future docility.

It could not be said that the meal was convivial. Umè-ko had received orders from her father not to appear. Tatsu's eyes, even as he ate, roamed ever along the corridors of the house, out to the garden, and pried at the closed edges of the fusuma. This restlessness brought to the host new apprehension. Such tension could not last. Tatsu must be enticed from the house.

After some hesitation and a spasmodic clearing of the throat, the old man asked, "Will you accompany me, young sir, upon a short walk to the city?"

"Why should I go to the city?"

"Ah—er—domo! it is, as you know, the centre of the universe, and has many wonderful sights,—great temples, theatres, wide shops for selling clothes—"

"I care nothing for these things."

"There are gardens, too; and a broad, shining river. Shall we not go to the autumn flowering garden of the Hundred Corners?"

"To such a place as that I would go alone,—or with her," said the boy, his disconcerting gaze fixed on the other's face. "When is the Dragon Maiden to appear?"

Kano looked down upon the matting. He cleared his throat again, drained a fresh cup of tea, and answered slowly, "Since she and I are of the city,—not the mountains,—and must abide in some degree by the city's social laws, you will not see her any more at all, unless it be arranged that you become her husband."

"And then,—if I become what you say,—how soon?" the other panted.

"I shall need to speak with the women of my house concerning this," said Kano in a troubled voice. He too, though Tatsu must not dream it, chafed at convention. He longed to set the marriage for next week,—next day, indeed,—and have the waiting over. Kano hated, of all things, to wait. Something might befall this untrained citizen at any hour,—then where would the future of the Kano name be found?

He had scarcely noted how the boy crouched and quivered in his place, as an animal about to spring. This indecision was a goad, a barb. Yet he was helpless! The memory of Umè's whispered words came back: "He, too, has power of the gods.... Believe, sir, that you, as I, are subject to his will." How could it be permitted of the gods that two beings like themselves,—fledged of divinity, touched with ethereal fire,—were under bondage to this wrinkled fox!

Tatsu flung himself sidewise upon the floor, and made as if to rise; then, in a dull reaction, settled back into his place. "You say she is not to come before me in this house to-day?"

"No, nor on other days, until your marriage."

"Then I go forth into the city,—alone," said the boy. He rose, but Kano stopped him.

"Wait! I shall accompany you, if but a little way. You do not know the roads. You will be lost!"

"I could return to this place from the under-rim of the world," said Tatsu. "Bound, crippled, blindfold,—I should come straight to it."

"Maybe, maybe," said Kano, "nevertheless I will go."

Tatsu would have defied him, outright, but Umè's words remained with him. Nothing mattered, after all, if he was some day to gain her. He must be patient, put a curb upon his moods! This was a fearful task for one like him, but he would strive for self-control just as one throws down a tree to bridge a torrent. After the Dragon Maid was won,—well then,—this halting insect man need not trouble them. They left the house together, Tatsu in scowling silence at the unwelcomed comradeship, Kano hard put to it to match his steps with the boy's long, swinging mountain stride.

"What am I to do with this wild falcon for a month?" thought Kano, half in despair, yet smiling, also, at the humor. "He must be clothed,—but how? I would sooner sheathe a mountain cat in silks! The one hope of existence during this interval is to get him engrossed in painting; but where is he to paint? I dare not keep him in the house with Umè, nor with old Mata, neither, for she might poison him. If only Ando Uchida had not gone away, leaving no address!"

Meantime, in the Kano home, Mata and Umè moved about in different planes of consciousness. The elder was still irritated by the morning's event. She considered it a personal indignity, a family outrage, that her master should walk the streets of Yeddo with a vagabond possessing neither hat nor shoes, and only half a kimono.

Each tended, as usual, her allotted household tasks. There was no change in the outer performance of the hours, but Mata remained alert, disturbed, and the girl tranquilly oblivious. The old face searching with keen eyes the young noted with troubled frown the frequent smile, the intervals of listless dreaming, the sudden starts, as by the prick of memory still new, and dipped in honey. There seemed to be in Umè-ko a gentle yearning for a human presence, though, to speak truly, Mata could not be certain that she was either heard or seen for fully one half of the time. The hour had almost reached the shadowless one of noon. Umè-ko's work was done. She had taken up her painting, only to put it listlessly to one side. The pretty embroidery frame met the same indignity. She sat now on the kitchen ledge, while Mata made the fire and washed the rice, toying idly with a white pebble chosen for its beauty from thousands on the garden path. Something in the childlike attitude, the placid, irresponsible face, brought the old servant's impatience to a climax. She deliberately hurled a dart.

"I suppose you know, Miss Umè, that your father may actually adopt this goblin from Kiu Shiu!"

"Ah, do you mean Sir Tatsu? Yes, I know. He, my father, has always longed to have a son."

"A son is desirable when the price is not too great," said the old dame, nodding sagely. "You are old enough to realize also, Miss Kano Umè-ko, what is the meaning of adoption into a family where there is a daughter of marriageable age."

Umè's face drooped over until the pebble caught a rosy glow. The old servant chuckled. "Eh, young mistress, you know what I mean? You are thinking of it?"

"I am trying very hard not to think of it," said Umè.

"Ma-a-a! And I have little wonder for that fact! Your father will sacrifice you without a tear,—he cares but for pictures. And Mata is helpless,—Mata cannot help her babe! Arà! It is a world of dust!"

"How old was my mother when she came here, Mata?"

"Just eighteen. Younger than you are now, my treasure."

"She was both beautiful and happy, you have said."

"Yes, both, both! Ah, how time speeds for the old. It seems but a short year or more that we two entered here together, she and I. From childhood I had nursed her. I thought your father old for her, in spite of his young heart and increasing fame. But he loved her truly, and has mourned for her. Even now he prays thrice daily before her ihai on the shrine. And she loved him,—almost too deeply for a woman of her class. She loved him, and was happy!"

"Only one year!" sighed Umè. "But it must be a great thing to be happy even for one year. Some people are not happy ever at all."

"One must not think of personal happiness,—it is wicked. Does not even your old mumbling abbot on the hill tell you so much? And now, of all times, do not start the dreaming. You will be sacrificed to art," said Mata, gloomily.

"Do I look like my mother, Mata San?"

The old dame wiped her eyes on her sleeve that she might see more clearly. Something in the girl's pure, upraised face caught at her heart, and the tears came afresh. "Wait," she whispered; "stay where you are, and you shall see your mother's face." She went into her tiny chamber, and from her treasures brought out a metal mirror given her by the young wife, Uta-ko. "Look,—close," she said, placing it in Umè's hand. "That is the bride of nineteen years ago. Never have you looked so like her as at this hour!"

Kano came back alone,—tired, dusty, and discouraged. Tatsu had escaped him, he said, at the first glimpse of the Sumida River. There was no telling when he might return,—whether he would ever return. To attempt control of Tatsu was like caging a storm in bamboo bars. Mata's eyes narrowed at this recital. "Yet I fervently thank the gods for him," said the speaker, sharply, in defiance of her look.

Restored to comparative serenity, Kano, later in the afternoon, sent for his daughter, and condescended to unfold to her those plans in which she played a vital part.

"Umè-ko, my child, you have always been a good and obedient daughter. I shall expect no opposition from you now," he began, in the manner of a patriarch.

Umè bowed respectfully. "Thank you, dear father. What has arisen that you think I may wish to oppose?"

"I did not say that I expected you to oppose anything. I said, on the contrary, it was something I expected you not to oppose."

"I await respectfully the words which shall tell me what it is I am not to oppose," said Umè-ko, quite innocently, with another bow. Kano put on his horn-rimmed spectacles. There was something about his daughter not altogether reassuring. His prearranged sentences began to slip away, like sand.

"I will speak briefly. I wish you to become the wife of the Dragon Painter, that we may secure him to the race of Kano. He has no name of his own. He is the greatest painter since Sesshu!" The speaker waved his hands. All had been said.

In the deep, following silence each knew that old Mata's ear felt, like a hand, at the crevice of the shoji.

"Father, are you sure,—have you yet spoken to—to—him," Umè-ko faltered at last. "Would he augustly condescend?"

"Condescend!" echoed the old man with a laugh. "Why, he demanded it last night, even in the first hour of meeting. He was angered that I did not give you up at once. He says you are his already. Oh, he is strange and wild, this youth. There are no reins to hold him, but—he is a painter!"

A grunt of derision came from the kitchen wall. Umè sat motionless, but her face was growing very pale.

"Well," said her father with impatience, "do you agree? And what is the earliest possible date?"

"I must consult with Mata," whispered the girl.

"She listens at the crack. Consult her now," said Kano.

The old dame threw aside the shoji like an armor, and walked in. "Yes, ask me what I think! Ask the old servant who has nursed Miss Umè from her birth, managed the house, scrubbed, haggled, washed, and broken her old bones for you! This is my advice,—freely given,—make of the youth her jinrikisha man, but not her husband!"

"Impertinent old witch!" cried Kano. "You are asked for nothing but the earliest possible date for the marriage!"

"Do you give yourself so tamely to a dangerous wild creature from the hills?" Mata demanded of the girl.

"Yes, yes, she'll marry him," said Kano, before her words could come. "The date,—the earliest possible hour! Will two weeks be too soon?"

"Two weeks!" shrieked the old dame, and staggered backward. "Is it of the scavenger's daughter that you speak?"

"Four weeks, then,—a month. It cannot be more. I tell you, woman, for a longer time than this I cannot keep the youth at bay. Is a month decent in convention's eyes?"

Mata began to sob loudly in her upraised sleeve.

"I see that it is at least permissible," said Kano, grimly. "What a weak set of social idiots we are, after all. Tatsu is right to scorn us! Well, well, a month from this date, deep in the golden heart of autumn, will the wedding be."

"If the day be propitious and the stars in harmony," supplemented Mata. "She shall not be married in the teeth of evil fortune, if I have to murder the Dragon Painter with my fish-knife!"

"Oh, go; have the stars arranged to suit you. Here's money for it!" He fumbled in his belt for a purse of coin, threw it to the mats, and, over the old dame's stooping back, motioned Umè-ko permission to withdraw. The girl went swiftly, thankful for the release.

"A good child,—a daughter to thank the gods for," chuckled Kano, as she left.

Mata looked sharply about, then leaned to her master's ear. "You are blind; you are an earth-rat, Kano Indara. This is not the usual submission of a silly girl. Umè is thinking things we know nothing of. Did you not see that her face was as a bean-curd in its whiteness? She kept so still, only because she was shaking in all directions at once. There, look at her now! She is fleeing to the garden with the uncertain step of one drunk with deep foreboding!"

"Bah! you are an old raven croaking in a fog! Go back to your pots. I can manage my own child!"

"You have never yet managed her or yourself either," was the spoiled old servant's parting shaft.

Kano sat watching the slender, errant figure in the garden. Yes, she had taken it calmly,—more calmly than he could have hoped. How beautiful was the poise, even at this distance, of the delicate throat, and the head, with its wide crown of inky hair! Each motion of the slow-strolling form in its clinging robes was a separate loveliness.

Kano drew a long sigh. He could not blind himself to Tatsu's savagery. This was not the sort of husband that Umè had a right to expect from her father's choice,—a youth not only penniless, and without family name, but in himself unusual, strange, with look, voice, gesture, coloring each a clear contrast to the men that Umè-ko had seen. He could not bear the thought of her unhappiness, and yet, at any sacrifice, Tatsu must be kept an inmate of their home.

The girl had stopped beside the sunlit pond, leaning far over. She did not seem to note the clustering carp at all, but rather dwell upon her own image, twisted and shot through with the gold of their darting bodies. Now, with dragging feet she went to the moon-viewing hill, remaining in the shadow of it, and pausing for long thought. Her eyes were on the cliff, now raised to the camphor tree. Suddenly she shivered and hid her face. What was the tumult of that ignorant young breast?

The old man rose and went to an inner room where hung the Butsudan, the shrine. He stood gazing upon the ihai of his wife. His lips moved, but the breath so lightly issued that the flame on the altar did not stir. "She, our one child, has come now to the borders of that woman-land where I cannot go with her," he was saying. "Thou art the soul to guide, and give her happiness, thou, the dear one of my life,—the dead young mother who has never really died!" He folded his hands now, and bowed his head. The small flame leaned to him. "Namu Amida Butsu, Namu Amida Butsu," murmured the old man.

Out by the hill, a butterfly, snow white, rested a moment on the young girl's hair. She was again looking at the cliff, and did not notice it.

V

Ando Uchida, from his green seclusion among the bamboo groves of Meguro, sent, from time to time, a scout into the city. First an ordinary hotel kotsukai or man-servant was employed. This experiment proved costly as well as futile. The kotsukai demanded large payment; and then the creature's questions to Mata were of a nature so crude and undiplomatic that they aroused instant suspicion, causing, indeed, the threat of a dipper of scalding water.

The next messenger was an insect peddler, Katsuo Takanaka by name. It was the part of this youth to search daily among the bamboo stems and hillside grasses of Meguro for the musical suzu-mushi, the hataori, and the kirigirisu. These he incarcerated in fairy cages of plaited straw, threaded the cages into great hornets' nests that dangled from the two ends of his creaking shoulder-pole, and started toward the city in a perfect storm of insect music. The noise moved with him like a cloud. It formed, as it were, a penumbra of fine shrilling, and could be heard for many streets in advance. This itinerant merchant was commissioned to haunt the Kano gate until impatience or curiosity should fling it wide for him. Then, after having coaxed old Mata into making a purchase, he was to engage her in conversation, and extract all the domestic information he could. Unfortunately for the acquisition of paltry news, it was Umè-ko, not Mata, who came out to purchase. The seller, watching those slim, white fingers as they fluttered among his cages, the delicate ear bent to mark some special chime, forgot the words of Ando Uchida, otherwise, Mr. S. Yetan, of Chikuzen, forgot everything, indeed, but the beauty of the girlish face near him.

He left the house in a dream more dense than the multitudinous clamor of his burden. "Alas!" thought Katsuo, as he stumbled along, unheeding the beckoning hands of mothers, or the arresting cries of children in many gateways, "Had I been born a samurai of old, and she an humble maiden! Even as an Eta, an outcast, would I have loved and sought her. Now in this life I am doomed to catch insects and to sell them. Perhaps in my coming rebirth, if I am honest and do not tell to the ignorant that a common mimi is a silver-voiced hataorimushi,—perhaps——"

Ando's third envoy was chosen with more thoughtful care. This time it was none other than a young priest from the temple of Fudo-Bosatsu in Meguro. He was an acolyte sent forth with bowl and staff to beg for aid in certain temple repairs. Ando promised a generous donation in return for information concerning the Kano family. Being assured that the motive for this curiosity was benevolent rather than mischievous, the priest consented to make the attempt. He reached the Kano gate at noon, within a few days after Tatsu's arrival. Mata opened to his call. Being herself a Protestant, opposed to the ancient orders and their methods, she gave him but a chilly welcome. Her interest was aroused, however, in spite of herself, by the fact that he neither chanted his refrain of supplication nor extended the round wooden bowl.

"I shall not entreat alms of money in this place," he said, as if in answer to her look of surprise, "I am weary, and ask but to rest for a while in the pleasant shade of your roof."

Without waiting for Mata's rejoinder, Umè-ko, who had heard the words of the priest, now came swiftly to the veranda. "Our home is honored, holy youth, by your coming," she said to him. "Enter now, I pray, into the main guest-room, where I and my father may serve you."

The priest refused this homage (much to Mata's inward satisfaction), saying that he desired only the stone ledge of the kitchen entrance and a cup of cold water.

After his first swift upward look he dared not raise his eyes again. The sweetness of her young voice thrilled and troubled him. But for his promise to Uchida he would have fled at once, as from temptation. Umè-ko, seeing his embarrassment, withdrew, but not until she had made an imperious gesture to old Mata, commanding her to serve him with rice and tea.

After a short struggle with himself the priest decided to accept the offer of food. Old Mata, he knew, was to be his source of information. The old dame served him in conscious silence. Her lips were compressed to wrinkled metal. The visitor, more accustomed to old women than to young, smiled at the rigid countenance, knowing that a loquacity requiring so obvious a latch is the more easily freed. He planned his first question with some care.

"Is this not the home of an artist, Kano by name?"

Mata tossed her gray hair. "Of the only Kano," she replied, and shut her lips with a snap.

"The only Kano, the only Kano," mused the acolyte over his tea.

"So I said, young sir. Is it that your hearing is honorably non-existent?"

"Then I presume he is without a son," said the priest as if to himself, and stirred the surmise into his rice with the two long wooden chopsticks Mata had provided.

The old dame's muscles worked, but she kept silence.

Umè-ko, now in her little chamber across the narrow passage, with a bit of bright-colored sewing on her knees, could hear each word of the dialogue. Mata's shrill voice and the priest's deep tones each carried well. The girl smiled to herself, realizing as she did the conflict between love of gossip and disapproval of Shingon priests that now made a paltry battlefield of the old dame's mind. The former was almost sure to win. The priest must have thought this, too, for he finished his rice in maddening tranquillity, and then stirred slightly as if to go. Mata's speech flowed forth in a torrent.

"My poor master has no son indeed, no true son of his house; but lately,—within this very week——" She caught herself back as with a rein, snatched up the empty tea-pot, hurried to the kitchen and returned partly self-conquered, if not content. She told herself that she must not gossip about the master's affairs with a beggarly priest. Determination hardened the wrinkles of her face.

If the priest perceived these new signs of taciturnity, he ignored them. "Your master being verily the great artist that you say, it is a thing doubly to be regretted that he is without an heir," persisted the visitor, with kind, boyish eyes upon old Mata's face. The old woman blinked nervously and began to examine her fingernails. "Alas!" sighed he, "I fear it is because this Mr. Kano is no true believer, that he has not prayed or made offerings to the gods."

Mata had a momentary convulsion upon the kitchen floor, and was still.

The priest kept gravity upon his mouth, but needed lowered lids to hide the twinkles in his eyes. "True religion is the greatest boon," he droned sententiously. "Would that your poor master had reached enlightenment!"

Umè-ko in her room forgot her sewing, and leaned a delicate ear closer to the shoji.

Old Mata's wall of reserve went down with a crash. "He believes as you believe!" she cried out shrilly. "All your Shingon chants and invocations and miracles he has faith in. Is that not what you call enlightenment? He and Miss Umè worship together almost daily at the great temple above us on the hill. The two finest stone lanterns there are given in the name of my master's dead young wife. Her ihai is in this house, and an altar, and they are well tended, I assure you! My master is a true believer, poor man, and what has his belief brought him? Ma-a-a! all this mummery and service and what has come of it?"

"I perceive with regret that you are not of the Shingon sect," remarked the priest.

"Me? I should say not!" snorted Mata. "I am a Protestant, a good Shinshu woman,—that's what I am, and I tell you so to your face! When I pray, I know what I am praying for. I trust to my own good deeds and the intercession of Amida Butsu. No muttering and mummery for me!"

"Ah!" said the priest, a most alluring note of interest now audible in his voice, "your master has so zealously importuned the gods, and, you say, with no result?"

"Ay, a result has come," answered the old dame, sullenly. "Within this week the gods—or the demons—have heard my master, for a wild thing from the hills is with us!"

"Wild thing? Do you mean a man?"

"A semblance of a man, though none such will you see in the streets of a respectable town."

"But does your master——" began the priest, in some perplexity.

Mata cut him short. "Because he can smear ink on paper with a brush, my master dotes on him and says he will adopt him!"

The woman's fierce sincerity transmitted vague alarm. Slipping his hands within his gray sleeves, the acolyte began fingering his short rosary as he asked, "Is the—wild man now under this very roof?"

"Not under a roof when he can escape it, you may be sure! He comes to us only when driven by hunger of the stomach or the eyes. Doubtless at this moment he wallows among the ferns and sa-sa grass of the mountain side, or lies face down in the cemetery near my mistress' grave. He is mad, my master is mad, and Miss Umè, if she really gives herself in marriage to the mountain lion, madder than all the rest!"

"That beautiful maiden whom I saw will be given to such a one?" asked the priest, in a startled way.

"Such are the present plans," said the other in deep despair, and huddled herself together on the floor.

Umè-ko, in her room across the hallway, had half risen. It really was time to check the old servant's vulgar garrulity. But the silence that followed the last remark checked her impulse. After all, what did it matter? No one could understand or needed to understand.

Meanwhile Mata, at first unconscious of anything but her own dark thoughts, became gradually aware of a strange look in the face of the priest. He, on his part, was wondering whether, indeed, the beauty of Umè-ko were not the sole cause of his patron's interest in the Kano family. After watching him intently for a few moments the old woman wriggled nearer and whispered in a tone so low that Umè could not catch the words, "Perhaps, after all, Sir Priest, you, being of their belief, perceive this to be a case where charms and spells are advisable. I am convinced that this house is bewitched, that the Dragon Painter has a train of elementals in attendance. Now, if we could only drive him forever from the place. Have you, by any chance, a powder, or an amulet, or a magic invocation you could give me?"

"No, no! I dare not!" said the other, in an agitated voice. He reached out for his bowl and, with a single leap, was down upon the earth. Mata caught him by his flying skirts. "See here," she entreated, "I will make it worth your while, young sir, I will give donations to your temple——"

"I dare not. I have no instructions to meddle with such things. Let me now give the house a blessing, and withdraw. But I can tell you for your comfort," he added, seeing the disappointment in her wrinkled face, "if, as you assure me, this is a house of faith, no presence entirely evil could dwell within it."

He got away before she could repeat her importunities; and the old dame returned to the kitchen, muttering anathemas against the mystic powers she had just attempted to invoke.

On the priest's return, Ando questioned him eagerly. He gained, almost with the first words, certainty of his own freedom. With Tatsu safely arrived, and the betrothal to Kano Umè-ko an outspoken affair, then had the time come for him—Ando Uchida—to reassume the pleasant role of friend and benefactor.

He moved into Yeddo before nightfall. His first visit was, of course, to Kano. Elaborately he explained to the sympathetic old man how he had been summoned by telegram into a distant province to attend the supposed death-bed of a relative, how that relative had, by a miracle, recovered. "So now," he remarked in conclusion, "I am again at your service, and shall take the part not only of nakodo in the coming marriage, but of temporary father and social sponsor to our unsophisticated bridegroom."

Certainly nothing could have been more opportune than Uchida's reappearance, or more welcome than his proposed assistance. Mata, indeed, hastened to give a whole koku of rice to the poor in thank-offering that one sensible person besides herself was now implicated in the wedding preparations.

Uchida justified, many times over, her belief in him. In the district near the Kano home he rented, in Tatsu's name, a small cottage, paying for it by the month, in advance. With Mata's assistance, not to mention a small colony of hirelings, the floors were fitted with new mats, the woodwork of the walls, the posts, and veranda floors polished to a mirror-like brightness, and even the tiny garden set with new turf and flowering plants. Tatsu was lured down from the mountain side and persuaded to remain at night and part, at least, of each day, in this little haven of coming joy.

A secluded room was fitted up as a studio, for his sole use. Here were great rectangles of paper, rolls of thin silk, stretching frames, water holders, multitudinous brushes, and all the exquisite pigment that Japanese love of beauty has drawn from water, earth, and air; delicate infusions of sea-moss, roots, and leaves, saucers of warm earth ground to a paste, precious vessels of powdered malachite, porphyry, and lapis lazuli. But the boy looked askance upon the expensive outlay. His wild nature resented so obvious a lure. It seemed unworthy of a Dragon Painter to accept this multitude of material devices. He had painted on flakes of inner bark, still quivering with the life from which he had rudely torn them. Visions limned on rock and sand had been the more precious for their impermanence. Here, every stroke was to be recorded, each passing whim and mood registered, as in a book of fate.

For days the little workroom remained immaculate. Kano began to fret. Ando Uchida, the wise, said, "Wait." It was Mata who finally precipitated the crisis. One rainy morning, being already in an ill humor over some trifling household affair, she was startled and annoyed by the sudden vision of Tatsu's head thrust noiselessly into her kitchen. Rudely she had slammed the shoji together, calling out to him that he had better be off doing the one thing he was fit to do, rather than to be skulking around her special domain. Tatsu had, as rudely, reopened the shoji panels, tearing a large hole in the translucent paper. "He had come merely for a glimpse of the Dragon Maid," he told the angry dame. "In a few days more she was to be his wife, and this maddening convention of keeping him always from her was eating out his vitals with red fire," so declared Tatsu, and let the consuming passion blaze in his sunken eyes.

But Mata, undismayed, stood up in scornful silence. She was gathering herself together like a storm, and in an instant more had hurled upon him the full terror of her vocabulary. She called him a barbarian, a mountain goat,—a Tengu,—better mated to a fox spirit or a she-demon than to a decent girl like her young mistress. She denounced her erstwhile beloved master as a blind old dotard, and the idolized Umè, she declared a weak and yielding idiot. Tatsu's attempts at retort were swept away with a hiss. For a while he raged like a flame upon the doorstep, but he was no match for his vigorous opponent. It was something to realize his own defeat. Gasping, he turned to the friendly rain and would have darted from the gate when, with a swoop like a falcon, Mata was bodily upon him. He threw his right arm upward as if to escape a blow, but the old dame did not belabor him. She was trying to thrust something hard and strange into his other hand. He glanced toward it. The last indignity of an umbrella! "Open it, madman!" she cried shrilly after him, "and hold your robe up; it is one of your new silk ones!"

Tatsu had never used an umbrella in his life. Now he opened it eagerly. Anything to escape that frightful voice! In the windy street he clutched at his fluttering skirts as he had seen other men do, and, with a last terrified backward glance, ran breathlessly toward the haven of his temporary home.

The little house was empty. Tatsu was thankful for so much. The rooms were already pre-haunted by dreams of Umè-ko. Tatsu felt the peace of it sink deep into his soul. Instinctively his wandering feet led him into the little painting room. As usual, the elaborate display of artist materials chilled him. After his recent exasperation he longed to ease his heart of a sketch, but obstinacy held him back. He sat down in the centre of the space. A bevy of small, squeaking sounds seemed to enclose him. It took him some moments to recognize them as the irritating rustling of his silken dress. He sprang to his feet, tore off the new and expensive girdle of brocade, flung it into one corner and the offending robe into another, and remained standing in the centre of the small space clad only in his short white linen under-robe.

He looked about, now, for a more congenial sheathing. If he could but find the tattered blue kimono worn during that upward journey from Kiu Shiu! Stained by berries and green leaves, torn by a thousand graceful vines,—for laundering only a few vigorous swirls in a running stream with a quick sun-drying on the river stones,—yet how comfortable, how companionable it was! There had been a blue something folded on the shelf of his closet. He found it, opened it wide in the air and would have uttered a cry of joy but for the changed look of it. Even this had not escaped Mata's desecrating hands! It was mended everywhere. The white darning threads grinned at him like teeth. Also it was washed and ironed, and smelled of foreign soap. For an instant he tore at it angrily, and was minded to destroy it, but the sense of familiarity held him. He wrapped it about him slowly and, with bent head, again seated himself upon the floor.

The rain now fell in quivering wires of dull light. The world was strung with them like a harp, and upon them the wind played a monotonous refrain. Against the wall near Tatsu stood a light framework of wood with the silk already stretched and dried for painting. At his other hand a brush slanted sidewise from a bowl of liquid ink. The boy's pulses leaped toward these things even while his lips curled in disdain at the shallow decoy. "So they expect to trap me, these geese and jailers who have temporary dominance over my life," thought he, in scorn. No, even though he now desired it of himself, he would not paint! Let him but gain his bride—then nothing should have power to sting or fret him. But, oh, these endless days and hours of waiting! They corroded his very thought as acid corrodes new metal. He felt the eating of it now.

A spasm of pain and anger distorted his face. He gave a cry, caught up suddenly the thick hake brush, and hurled it across the room toward the upright frame of silk. It struck the surface midway, a little to the left; pressed and worked against it as though held by a ghost, and then, falling, dragged lessening echoes of stain.

Tatsu's mirthless laugh rang out against the sound of dripping rain. The childish outburst had been of some relief. He looked defiantly toward the white rectangle he had just defaced. Defaced? The boy caught in his breath. He thrust his head forward, leaning on one hand to stare. That bold and unpremeditated stroke had become a shadowed peak; the trailing marks of ink a splendid slope. Had he not seen just such a one in Kiu Shiu,—had he not scaled it, crying aloud upon its summit to the gods to yield him there his bride?

Trembling now, and weak, he crawled on hands and knees toward the frame. He had forgotten Kano, Uchida, Mata,—forgotten even Umè-ko. Fingers not his own lifted the fallen brush. The wonderful cold wind of a dawning frenzy swept clean his soul. He shivered; then a sirocco of fire followed the void of the wind. The spot where his random blow had struck still gleamed transparent jet. He dragged the blackened brush through a vessel of clear water, then brandished it like the madman Mata thought him. With the soft tuft of camel hair he blurred against the peak pale, luminous vapor of new cloud. Turning, twisting sidewise, this way, then that, the yielding implement, he seemed to carve upon the silk broad silver planes of rock, until there rose up a self-revealing vision, the granite cliff from which a thin, white waterfall leaps out.

"With the soft tuft of camel hair he blurred against the peak pale, luminous vapor of new cloud." Page 124.

"With the soft tuft of camel hair he blurred against the peak pale, luminous vapor of new cloud."

But this one swift achievement only whetted the famished appetite to more creative ardor. Sketch after sketch he made, some to tear at once into strips, others to fling carelessly aside to any corner where they might chance to fall, others, again, to be stored cunningly upon some remote shelf to which old Kano and Uchida and Mata could not reach, but whence he, Tatsu, the Dragon Painter, should, in a few days more, withdraw them and show them to his bride. The purple dusk brimmed his tiny garden, and yet he could not stop. Art had seized him by the throat, and shook him, as a prey. Uchida, peering at him from between the fusuma, perceived the glory and turned away in silence; nor for that day nor the next would he allow any one to approach the frenzied boy. The elder man had, himself in youth, fared along the valleys of art, and knew the signals on the peaks.

Tatsu, unconscious that the house was not still empty, painted on. Sometimes he sobbed. Again an ague of beauty caught him, and he needed to hurl himself full length upon the mats until the ecstacy was past. Just as the daylight went he saw, upon the one great glimmering square of silk as yet immaculate, a dream of Umè-ko, the Dragon Maiden, who had danced before him. This was an apparition too holy to be limned in artificial light. When the sun came, next day, he knew well what there was for him to do. He placed the frame upright, where the first pink beam would find it. Brushes, water vessels, and paints were placed in readiness, with such neatness and precision that old Kano's heart would have laughed in pleasure. That night the shoji and amado were not closed. Tatsu did not sleep. It was a night of consecration. He walked up and down, sometimes in the narrow room, sometimes in the garden. Often he prayed. Again he sat in the soft darkness, before the ghostly glimmer of the silk, tracing upon it visions of ethereal light. When, at last, the dawn came in, Tatsu bowed to the east, with his usual prayer of thankful piety, then, with the exaltation still upon him, lifted the silver thread of a brush and drew his first conscious outline of the woman soon to be his wife.

"He walked up and down, sometimes in the narrow room, sometimes in the garden." Page 126.

"He walked up and down, sometimes in the narrow room, sometimes in the garden."

VI

Through all these busy days Umè-ko moved as one but little interested. Kano and Uchida noticed nothing unusual. To them she was merely the conventional nonenity of maidenhood that Japanese etiquette demanded. It never entered their heads that she would not have agreed with equal readiness to any other husband of their choosing.

Mata knew her idol and nursling better. Hints of character and of deep-sea passion had risen now and again to the surface of the girl's placid life. There were currents underneath that the father did not suspect. Once, during her childhood, a pet bird had been injured in a fit of anger by old Kano. Umè-ko, with her ashen face under perfect control, had killed the suffering creature and carried it, wrapped in white paper, to her own room. The father, ashamed now, and filled with genuine remorse, had stormed up and down the garden paths, reviling himself for an impatient ogre, and promising more restraint in future. Mata, silent for once, had crept to her child-mistress' close-shut walls, heard the last sobbing words of a Buddhist prayer for the dead, and burst through the shoji in scant time to catch back the stroke of a dagger from the girl's slim, upraised throat. Her terrified screams summoned Kano and the neighbors as well. A priest hurried down from the temple on the hill. In time the culprit was reduced to a condition of tearful penitence, and gave her promise never again to attempt so cowardly and wicked a thing as self-destruction, unless it were for some noble and impersonal end.

The good old priest, to comfort her, chanted a sutra over the bier of her lost playmate, and bestowed upon it a high-sounding Buddhist kaimyo which Kano carved, in his finest manner, upon a wooden grave post. In time, the artist forgot the episode. Mata never forgot. Often in the long hours she thought of it now as she watched the girl's face bent always so silently above the bridal sewing. No impatience or regret were visible in her. Yet, thought Mata, surely no maiden in her senses could really wish to become the wife of an ill-mannered, untamed mountain sprite! Could Death be the secret of this pale tranquillity? Was Umè-ko to cheat them all, at the last, by self-destruction?

In such wise did the old servant fret and ponder, but no assurance came. A true insight into art might have opened many doors to her. Yet, through a life devoted to the externals of it, Mata had been tolerant of beauty, rather than at one with it. The impractical view of life which art seemed to demand of its devotees was enough to arouse suspicion, if not her actual dislike. Uchida was a hero because he had been bold enough to shake himself free from lethargic influences, and achieve a shining and substantial success.

But even had the key of art been thrust into the old dame's groping hand, and even had her master guided her, there was an inner chamber of Umè's heart which they could not have found. Umè herself had not known of it until that first instant when, now three weeks ago, a strange young face, hung about with shadows, had peered into her father's gate. With the first sound of his voice, she had entered in, had knelt before a shrine whereon, wrapped in fire, a Secret lay. Ever since she had needed to guard that shrine, not, indeed, for fear that the light would falter, but rather that it might not leap up, and lay waste her being. As one guards a flame, so Umè-ko, with silence and prayer and self-enforced tranquillity, guarded the sacred spark from winds of passion. Each day at dawn, and again at twilight of each day, it flamed high and was hard to conquer, for with dawn a letter was hers—held in the night-wet branches of her dragon-plum, and each night when Mata and her father thought her sleeping, an answer was written, and committed to the keeping of the tree.

When Tatsu did not paint, or rest from sheer exhaustion, he was writing. Umè, bending above his words, shivering at times, or weeping, marvelled that the tissue had not charred beneath the thoughts burned into it. Tatsu's phrases were like his paintings, unusual, vital, almost demoniac in force, shot through and through at times with the bolt of an almost unbearable beauty. Her own words answered his, as the tree-tops answer storm, with music. Verse alone could ease the girl of her ecstacy, and each recorded and triumphed in the demolition of yet another day. "Another stone, beloved, thrust down from the dungeon wall that severs us!"

Swiftly the heap of wedding garments grew. There were delicate kimonos, as thin and gray as mist, with sunset-colored inner robes of silk; gowns of linen and cotton for indoor wear; bath and sleeping robes with great designs of flowers, birds, or landscapes; silken bed-quilts and bright floor cushions; great sashes crusted like bark with patternings of gold; dainty toilet accessories of hairpins, girdles, collarettes, shopping-bags, purses, jewel-cases,—and new sandals of various sorts, each with velvet thongs of some delicate hue.

The sewing was, of course, done at home. Mata would have trusted this sacred rite to no domination but her own. She worked incessantly, planning, cutting, scolding,—hurrying off to the shopping district for some forgotten item, conferring with Ando Uchida about the details of Tatsu's outfit, then returning, flushed with success and importance, to new home triumphs.

Umè sewed steadily all day. Her painting materials had been put meekly aside, and, as a further precaution at old Mata's hands, hidden under the kitchen flooring. Toward the last it was found necessary to employ an assistant, a seamstress, known of old to Mata. Her companionship, as well as her sewing, proved a boon. Seated upon the springy matting, with waves of shimmering silk tumultuous about them, the old dames chatted incessantly of other brides and other wedding outfits they had known. Marvellous were their tales of married life, some of them designed to cheer, others to warn the silent little third figure, that of the bride-to-be. As a matter of fact, Umè never listened. The noise and buzz of incessant conversation affected her pleasantly, but remotely, as the chatter of distant sparrows. The girl had too much within herself to think of.

"May Kwannon have mercy upon my young mistress," sighed the nurse, one day, as Umè left the room.

"Does she require mercy? I thought—she appears to me honorably—er—undisturbed," ventured the seamstress, with one swift upward look of interest.

"Yes, she appears,—many of us appear,—but can she be happy? That is what I wish to know. The creature she is being forced to marry is more like a mountain-lion than a man!"

"Ma-a-a! Is he dangerous? Will he bite her?" questioned the other, hopefully.

"Amida alone knows what he will do with her," croaked Mata, in a sepulchral voice.

The subject was one not to be readily relinquished. "The facts being honorably as you relate," began the hired seamstress, her needle held carefully against the light for threading, "how is it that the august father of the illustrious young lady permits such a marriage?"

Mata's eyes gleamed sharp and bright as the needle. "Because he is as mad as the wild man, and all for pictures! They would strip their own skins off if that made better parchment. Miss Umè has been influenced by them, and now is to be sacrificed. Alas! the evil day!" and Mata wiped away some genuine tears on the hem of a night-robe she had finished.

"O kinodoku Sama, my spirit is poisoned by your grief," murmured the other, sympathetically. "Yet, in your place, I should find great comfort in the outfit of your mistress. Never, even in the sewing halls of princes, could more beautiful silks be gathered." She looked about slowly, with the air of a professional who sees something really worthy of regard.

Mata's face cleared. "Since the gods allow it, I should not complain," she admitted. "Indeed, Mr. Uchida and I are doing well by the young couple in the matter of silks and house furnishings. And—whisper this not—no one but he and I dream from what source these splendid fabrics come!"

Mata had thrust a poisoned arrow of curiosity into her listener, and knew it. Some day, perhaps the very day before the wedding, she might reveal it. For the present, as she said, no one but herself and Uchida knew.

More than once during sewing hours, Umè-ko herself had wondered how her father was able to give her silks of such beauty and variety. With the unthrift of the true artist, Kano was always poor. The old man would have been as surprised and far angrier than his daughter, had he known that Tatsu's pictures, stolen craftily by the confederates, Uchida and Mata, and sold in Yokohama for about a tenth of their true value, were the source of this sudden affluence. Tatsu remained ignorant, also. But, provided they took no image of Umè's face, he would not have cared at all. New garments, new mats, dainty household furnishings, were showered upon him, too; but they might have been autumn leaves, for all the interest he showed.

To gain his Dragon Maid,—to know that in this life she was irrevocably his,—that was Tatsu's one conscious thought.

The wedding day came at last. Umè-ko had written no letter on the eve of it, but all night long she felt that he was near her, leaning on the breast of the plum tree, scaling the steeps above her, wandering, a restless ghost of joy, about the moon-silvered cemetery, speaking perhaps, as equal, to his primeval gods. So close, already were these two, that even in absence, each felt always something of the other's mood. It was a sleepless night to the girl, also. She cowered close about the Secret, until its fierce light scorched her. She pressed down her lids with strong, white fingers, but the glory streamed through. So, tortured by intolerable bliss, she suffered, until the dawn came in.

Quite early in the day the bride's trousseau and gifts were sent to Tatsu's home. They made a train that filled the neighbors' eyes with wonder and Mata's swelling heart with pride. There were lacquered chests and cases of drawers, all filled with clothing. Each great square package was covered with a decorated cloth, and swung from a gilded staff borne on the shoulders of two stout coolies. There were boxes of cakes, fruit, and eggs; and jinrikishas piled with a medley of gifts. Even Kano was impressed. Uchida rubbed his two fat hands together and laughed at everything. Umè-ko, watching the moving shadows pass under her father's gate-roof, closed her eyes quickly and caught her breath. The next gift from the Kano home was to be herself.

By this time autumn was upon the year. A few early chrysanthemums opened small golden suns in the garden. Dodan bushes and maples hinted at a crimson splendor soon to follow. The icho trees stood like pyramids of gold; and suzuki grass upon the hillsides brushed a cloudless blue sky with silken fingers. In the garden, autumn insects sang. Umè-ko's kirigirisu which, some weeks before, she had released from its cage, had, as if in gratitude made a home among the lichens of the big plum tree. Umè believed that she always knew its voice from among the rest, no matter how full the chorus of silver chiming.

She had gone back to her room, and sat now, in the centre of it, staring toward the garden. Noon had crept upon it, devouring all shadow. Her eyes saw little but the golden blur. A fusuma opened softly, and two women, Mata and the attendant seamstress, came mincing and smirking toward her, each with an armful of white silk. Umè rose like an automaton. They began her toilet, talking the while in low voices. They robed her in white with a thin lining-edge of crimson, and threw over her shining hair a veil of tissue. Some one outside called that the bride's kuruma was at the gate. Old Kano entered the room, smiling. His steps creaked and rustled with new silk. Umè turned for one fleeting glimpse of her plum tree. It seemed to stir and wave green leaves toward her. With head down-bent, the girl followed her father through the house.

Mata helped them into the two new, shining jinrikishas, a dragon-crest blazoned on the one for Umè's use. She scolded the kuruma men in her shrill voice, giving a dozen instructions in one sentence, and pretending anger at their answering jests. On the doorstep stood the little seamstress ready to cast a handful of dried peas. When Kano and Umè-ko were off, Mata scrambled excitedly into her own vehicle. Her human steed, turning round for an impudent and good-natured stare, drawled out an unprintable remark. The seamstress shrieked "sayonara" and pelted space with the peas. Afterward she ran on foot down the slope of the hill and joined the smiling crowd of lookers-on. Soon it was over. The peddler picked up his pack, and the children their toys. Gates opened or slid aside in panels to receive their owners. The jangling of small gate-bells made the hillside merry for an instant, then busy silence again took possession.

No one at all was left in the Kano home. The little cottage of Umè's birth, of her short, happy life and dawning fame, drew itself together in the unusual silence. Sunshine fell thick upon the garden, and warmed even the lazy gold-fish in their pigmy lake. In the plum-tree branch that touched Umè-ko's abandoned chamber, the cricket chirped softly to himself. He knew the Secret!

VII

Six days were gone. The marriage was a thing accomplished, yet old Kano sat, lean, dispirited, drowned apparently in depths of fathomless despair, in the centre of his corner room. Mata, busy about her household tasks, sometimes passed across the matting, or flaunted a dusting-cloth within a partly opened shoji. At such moments her look and gesture were eloquent of disdain. Her patience, long tried by the kindly irritable master, was about at an end. Surely a spoiled old man-child like the crouching figure yonder would exhaust the forbearance of Jizo Sama himself!

Six days ago he had been happy,—indeed, too happy! for he and Uchida had drunk themselves into a condition of giggling bliss, and had needed to be taken away bodily from the bridal bower, hoisted into a double jinrikisha, and driven off ignominiously, still embracing, still pledging with tears an eternity of brotherhood. Yes, on that day Kano had hailed the earth as one broad, enamelled sakè-cup, the air, a new infusion of heavenly brew. But now——

"Mata!" the thin voice came, "are you certain that this is but the sixth day of my son's wedding?"

"It is but the sixth day, indeed, since your daughter's sacrifice to a barbarian, if that is what you mean," returned Mata, with a belligerent flourish of her paper duster.

"That is what I meant," said the other, passively. "Then the week is not to be finished until to-morrow at noon. Twenty-four hours of torture to me! I suppose that the ingrates will count time to the last shadow! Oh, Mata, Mata, you once were a faithful servant! Why did you let me make that foolish promise of giving them an entire week? A day would have been ample, then Tatsu and I could have begun to paint."

"Ara!" said Mata, uttering a sound more forcible than respectful. "Had it been a decent person thus married to my young mistress, instead of a mountain sprite, they should have had a month together!"

Kano groaned under the suggestion. "Then, heartless woman, at the end of the month you would have been without a master; for surely my sufferings would, in a month, have shrunk me to an insect gaki chirping from a tree."

"It is to me a matter of honorable amazement that in one week you are not already a gaki, with your incessant complaints," retorted the old dame, still unrelenting.

"If I could be sure he is painting all this interminable time," said Kano to himself, wringing the nervous hands together.

"You may be augustly sure he is not," chuckled the cruel Mata.

The old man got hastily to his feet. "Mata, Mata, your tongue is that of a viper,—a green viper, with stripes. I will go from its reach into the highway. Of course my son is painting. What else could he be doing?"

The old dame's laugh fell like salt upon a wound. Kano caught up a bamboo cane and, hatless, went into the street. It was odd, how often during this week he found need of walking; still stranger, how often his wanderings led him to the dodan hedge enclosing Tatsu's cottage. He paused at the gate now, tormented by the reflection that he himself had drawn the bolt. How still it was in there! Not even a sparrow chirped. Could something be wrong? Suddenly a laugh rang out,—the low spontaneous laugh of a happy girl. Kano clutched the gate-post. It was not the sort of laugh that one gives at sight of a splendid painting. It had too intimate, too personal, a ring. But surely Tatsu was painting! What else did he live for, if not to paint? The old man bore a heavy homeward heart.

Next day, exactly at the hour of noon, the culprits tapped upon Kano's wooden gate. During the morning the old man had been in a condition of feverish excitement, but now that the agony of waiting had forever ceased, he assumed a pose of indifference.

Tatsu entered first, as a husband should. In mounting the stone which served as step to the railless veranda, he shook off, carelessly, his wooden shoes. Umè-ko lifted them, dusted the velvet thongs, and placed them with mathematical precision side by side upon the flat stone. She then entered, placing her small lacquered clogs beside those of her husband.

Kano, from the tail of his eye, marked with approval these tokens of wifely submission. From a small aperture in the kitchen shoji, however (a peephole commanding a full view of the house), dour mutterings might have been heard, and a whispered lament that "she should have lived to see her young mistress wipe a Tengu's shoes!"

When the various genuflections and phrases of ceremonial greeting were at last accomplished, the old artist broke forth, "Well, well, son Tatsu, how many paintings in all this time?"

Tatsu looked up startled, first at the questioner, then at his wife. She gave a little, convulsive giggle, and bent her shining eyes to the floor.

"I have not painted," said Tatsu, bluntly.

"Not painted? Impossible! What then have you done with all the golden hours of these interminable days?"

A sullen look crept into the boy's face. Again he turned questioning eyes upon his wife. From the troubled silence her sweet voice reached like a caress: "Dear father, the autumn days, though golden, have held unusual heat."

"Heat! What are cold and heat to a true artist? Did he not paint in August? I am old, yet I have been painting!"

Again fell the silence.

"I said that I had been painting," repeated the old man, angrily.

Umè-ko recovered herself with a start. "I am—er—we are truly overjoyed to hear it. Shall you deign to honor us with a sight of your illustrious work?"

"No, I shall not deign!" snapped the old man. "It is his work that you now are concerned with." Here he pointed to the scowling Tatsu. "Why have you not influenced him as you should? He must paint! It is what you married him for."

Umè-ko caught her breath. A flush of embarrassment dyed her face, and she threw a half-frightened look towards Tatsu. Answering her father's unrelenting frown, she murmured, timidly, "To-morrow, if the gods will, my dear husband shall paint."

Tatsu's steady gaze drew her. "Your eyes, Umè-ko. Is it true that for this—to make me paint—you consented to become my wife?"

Umè tried in vain to resist the look he gave her. Close at her other hand, she knew, her father hung upon her face and listened, trembling, for her words. To him, art was all. But to her and Tatsu, who had found each other,—ah! She tried to speak but words refused to form themselves. She tried to turn a docile face toward old Kano; but the deepening glory of her husband's look drew her as light draws a flower. Sullenness and anger fell from him like a cloth. His countenance gave out the fire of an inward passion; his eyes—deep, strange, strong, magnetic—mastered and compelled her.

"No, no, beloved," she whispered. "I cannot say,—you alone know the soul of me."

A fierce triumph flared into his look. He leaned nearer, with a smile that was almost cruel in its consciousness of power. Under it her eyes drooped, her head fell forward in a sudden faintness, her whole lithe body huddled into one gracious, yielding outline. Even while Kano gasped, doubting his eyes and his hearing, Tatsu sprang to his feet, went to his wife, caught her up rudely by one arm, and crushed her against his side, while he blazed defiant scorn upon Kano. "Come Dragon Wife," he said, in a voice that echoed through the space; "come back to our little home. No stupid old ones there, no prattle about painting. Only you and I and love."

"'Come, Dragon Wife,' he said, 'come back to our little home.'"
Page 150.

"'Come, Dragon Wife,' he said, 'come back to our little home.'"

Now in Japan nothing is more indelicate, more unpardonable, or more insulting to the listener than any reference to the personal love between man and wife. At Tatsu's terrible speech, Umè-ko, unconscious of further cause of offense, hid her face against his sleeve, and clung to him, that her trembling might not cast her to the floor. Kano, at first, was unable to speak. He grew slowly the hue of death. His brief words, when at last they came, were in convulsive spasms of sound. "Go to your rooms,—both. Are you mad, indeed,—this immodesty, this disrespect to me. Mata was right,—a Tengu, a barbarian. Go, go, ere I rise to slay you both!"

The utterance choked him, and died away in a gasping silence. He clutched at his lean chest. Umè would have sped to him, but Tatsu held her fast. His young face flamed with an answering rage. "Do you use that tone to me—old man—to me, and this, my wife," he was beginning, but Umè put frantic hands upon his lips.

"Master, beloved!" she sobbed. "You shall not speak thus to our father,—you do not understand. For love of me, then, be patient. Even the crows on the hilltops revere their parents. Come there, to the hills, with me, now, now—oh, my soul's beloved—before you speak again. Wait there, in the inner room, while I kneel a moment before our father. Oh, Tatsu, if you love me——"

The agony of her face and voice swept from Tatsu's mind all other feeling. He stood in the doorway, silent, as she threw herself before old Kano, praying to him as to an offended god: "Father, father, do not hold hatred against us! Tatsu has been without kindred,—he knows not yet the sacred duties of filial love. We will go from your presence now until your just anger against us shall have cooled. With the night we shall return and plead for mercy and forgiveness. No, no, do not speak again, just yet. We are going, now, now. Oh, my dear father, the agony and the shame of it! Sayonara, until the twilight." She hurried back to Tatsu, seized his clenched hand with her small, icy fingers, and almost dragged him from the room.

Kano sat as she had left him, motionless, now, as the white jade vase within the tokonoma. His anger, crimson, blinding at the first possession, had heated by now into a slow, white rage. All at once he began to tremble. He struck himself violently upon one knee, crying aloud, "So thus love influences him! Ara! My Dragon Painter! Other methods may be tried. Such words and looks before me, me,—Kano Indara! And Umè's eyes set upon him as in blinding worship. Could I have seen aright? He caught my child up like a common street wench, a thing of sale and barter. And she,—she did not scorn, but trembled and clung to him. Is the whole world on its head? I will teach them, I will teach them."

"Have my young mistress and her august spouse already taken leave?" asked Mata at a crack of the door.

"Either they or some demon changelings," answered the old man, rocking to and fro upon the mats.

The old servant had, of course, heard everything. Feigning now, for her own purposes, a soothing air of ignorance, she glided into the room, lifted the tiny tea-pot, shook it from side to side, and then cocked her bright eyes upon her master. "The tea-pot. It is honorably empty. Shall I fill it?"

"Yes, yes; replenish it at once. I need hot tea. Shameless, incredible; he has, indeed, the manners of a wild boar."

"Ma-a-a!" exclaimed the old woman. "Now of whom can my master be speaking?"

"You know very well of whom I am speaking, goblin! Do you not always listen at the shoji? Go, fill the pot!"

Mata glided from the room with the quickness of light and in an instant had returned. Replacing the smoking vessel and maintaining a face of decorous interest, she asked, hypocritically, "And was my poor Miss Umè mortified?"

"Mortified?" echoed the artist with an angry laugh; "she admired him! She clung to him as a creature tamed by enchantment. My daughter! Never did I expect to look upon so gross a sight! Why, Mata——"

"Yes, dear master," purred the old dame encouragingly as she seated herself on the floor near the tea-pot. "One moment, while I brew you a cup of fresh, sweet tea. It is good to quiet the honorable nerves. I can scarcely believe what you tell me of our Umè-ko, so modest a young lady, so well brought up!"

"I tell you what these old eyes saw," repeated Kano. Once more he described the harrowing sight, adding more details. Mata, well used to his outbursts of anger, though indeed she had seldom seen him in his present condition of indignant excitement, drew him on by degrees. She well knew that an anger put into lucid words soon begins to cool. Some of her remarks were in the nature of small, kindly goads.

"Remember, master, the poor creatures are married but a week to-day."

"Had I dreamed of such low conduct, they should never have been married at all!"

"Of course he is n't worthy of her," sighed the other, one eye on Kano's face.

"Nonsense! He is more than worthy of any woman upon earth if he could but learn to conduct himself like a human being."

"That would take a long schooling."

"He is the greatest artist since Sesshu!" cried the old man, vehemently.

Mata bowed over to the tea-pot. "You recognize artists, master; I recognize fools."

"Do you call my son a fool?"

"If that wild man is still to be considered your son, then have I called your son a fool," answered Mata, imperturbably.

The new flush left the old man's face as quickly as it had come. "Mata, Mata," he groaned, too spent now for further vehemence, "you are an old cat,—an old she-cat. You cannot dream what it is to be an artist! What one will endure for art; what one will sacrifice, and joy in the giving! Why, woman, if with one's shed blood, with the barter of one's soul, a single supreme vision could be realized, no true artist would hesitate. Yes, if even wife, child, and kindred were to be joined in a common destruction for art's sake, the artist must not hesitate. At the thought of one's parents, the ancestors of one's house, it might be admissible to pause, but at nothing else, nothing else, whatever! Life is a mere bubble on the stream of art, fame is a bubble—riches, happiness, Death itself! Would that I could tear these old limbs into a bleeding frenzy as I paint, if by doing so one little line may swerve the nearer to perfection! Often have I thought of this and prayed for the opportunity, but such madness does not benefit. Only the torn anguish of a soul may sometimes help. And with old souls, like old trees, they do not bleed, but are snapped to earth, and lie there rotting. He, Tatsu, the son of my adoption, could with one strong sweep of his arm make the gods stare, and he spends his hours fondling the perishable object of a woman, while I, who would give all, all,—give my own child that he loves,—I remain impotent! Alas! So topsy-turvy a world are we born in!"

He bowed his head in a misery so abject that Mata forbore to jibe. She tried to speak again, to comfort him, but he motioned her away, and sat, scarcely moving in his place, until the night brought Tatsu and his young wife home again.

VIII

Thus under, as it were, a double ban of displeasure, did the new generation of Kano, Tatsu and Umè-ko, begin life in the little cottage beneath the hill. They were given Umè's chamber near which the plum tree grew, an adjoining room having been previously fitted up for Tatsu's painting. As in the other cottage, inviting rectangles of silk, already stretched and sized, stood in blank rows against the walls. Even the fusuma were of new paper, offering, it would seem, to any inspired young artist, a surface of alluring possibilities. Paints, brushes, and vessels without number made an array to tempt, if only the tempting were not so obvious.

Umè-ko, watching closely the expression of her husband's face as he was first led into this room, drew old Kano aside, and urged that more tact and delicacy be used in leading Tatsu back to a desire for creative work. She herself, she hinted with deprecating sweetness, might do much if only allowed to follow her own loving instincts. But Kano had lost confidence in his daughter and bluntly told her so. Tatsu had been adopted and married in order to make him paint, and paint he should! Also it was Umè-ko's duty to influence him in whatever way and method her father thought best. Let her succeed,—that was her sole responsibility. So blustered Kano to himself and Mata, and not even the malicious twinkle of the old servant's eye pointed the way to wisdom.

Naturally Umè-ko did not succeed. Tatsu merely laughed at her flagrant efforts at duplicity. He felt no need of painting, no desire to paint. He had won the Dragon Maiden. Life could give him no more! There was no anger or resentment in his feeling toward Kano, or even the old scourge Mata. No, he was too happy! To lie dreaming on the fragrant, matted floor near Umè, where he could listen to her soft breathing and at times pull her closer by a silken sleeve,—this was enough for Tatsu. Nothing had power to arouse in him a sense of duty, of obligation to himself, or to his adopted father. He would not argue about it, and could scarcely be said to listen. He lived and moved and breathed in love as in a fourth dimension. To the old man's frequent remonstrances he would turn a gentle, deprecating face. He had promised Umè-ko never again to speak rudely to their father. Besides, why should he? The outer world was all so beautiful and sad and unimportant. A sunset cloud, or a bird swinging from a hagi spray could bring sharp, swift tears to his eyes. Beauty could move him, but not old Kano's genuine sufferings. Yet, the old man, bleating from the arid rocks of age, was doubtless a pathetic spectacle, and must be listened to kindly.

...e boy thus obdurate, Kano turned the full force of his ... Umè-ko. She endured in silence the incessant railing. Each ...ged by the distracted Kano she carried out with scrupulous ...even with the performance of it she knew hopelessness to be ...r hours she remained away from home, hidden in a neighbor's ... the temple on the hill, it being Kano's thought that perhaps, in this temp... rary loss of his idol, Tatsu might seek solace in the paint room. But Tatsu, raging against the conditions which made such tyranny possible, stormed, on such occasions, through the little house, and up and down the garden, pelting the terrified gold-fish in their caves, stripping leaves and tips from Kano's favorite pine-shrubs, or standing, long intervals of time, on the crest of the moon-viewing hillock, from which he could command vistas of the street below.

"There 's your jewel of a painter," old Mata, indoors, would say. "Look at him, master,—a noble figure, indeed, standing on one leg like a love-sick stork!" And Kano, helpless before his own misery and the old dame's acrid triumph, would keep silence, only muttering invocations to the gods for self-control.

Often the young wife pretended a sudden desire for her own artistic work. She would go hurriedly to the little painting chamber, gather complex paraphernalia, and assume the pose of eager effort. Tatsu always followed her but, once within the room, bent such laughing eyes of comprehension that she dared not look into his face. Nevertheless she would paint; tracing, mechanically, the bird and flower studies in which she had once taken delight. Just in the midst of some specially delicate stroke, Tatsu would snatch her hands away, press them against his lips, his eyes, his throat, hurl the painting things to the four corners of the room, drag her down to his strong embrace, and triumph openly in the victory of love. The young wife, longing from the first to yield, attempted always to repel him, protesting in the words her father had bade her use, and urging him to rouse himself and paint, as she was doing. Then the young god would laugh magnificent music, drowning the last pathetic echo of old Kano's remembered voice. Catching her anew he would crush her against his breast, fondling her with that tempestuous gentleness that surely no mere man of earth could know, would drag up her faint soul to him through eyes and lips until she felt herself but a shred of ecstacy caught in a whirlwind of immortal love.

> "So that we be together,
> Even the Hell of the Blood Lake,
> Even the Mountain of Swords,
> Mean nothing to us at all!"

He would sing, in the words of an old Buddhist folk-song. At such supreme heights of emotion she knew, consciously, that Kano's grief and disappointment were nothing. She did not really care whether Tatsu ever touched a brush again,—whether, indeed, the whole visible world fretted itself into dust. She and Tatsu had found each other! The rest meant nothing at all!

Such moments were, however, the isolated and the exceptional. As the days went by they became less frequent, and, by a strange law of contrasts, with diminution exacted a heavier toll. The strain of antagonisms within the little home became almost unbearable. Neither Kano nor Tatsu would yield an inch, and between them, like a white flower between stones, little Umè-ko was crushed. A new and threatening trouble was that of poverty. Tatsu would not paint; Kano, in his wretchedness could not.

The young wife went often now to the temple on the hill. Tatsu generally went with her, remaining outside in the courtyard or at the edge of the cliff, under the camphor tree, while she was praying within. Her entreaties were all for divine guidance. She implored of the gods a deeper insight into the cause of this strange trouble now upon them, and besought, too, that in her husband, Tatsu, should be awakened a recognition of his duties, and of the household needs. Kano visited the temple, also, and spent long hours in conference with his personal friend, the abbot. Even old Mata, abandoning for the moment her Protestantism and reverting to the yearning (never entirely stifled) for mystic practises, went to an old charlatan of a fortune-teller, and purchased various charms and powders for driving the demons from the unconscious Tatsu. Umè-ko soon discovered this, and the fear that Tatsu would be poisoned added to a load of anxiety already formidable.

By the end of October, Yeddo's most golden and most perfect month, no hours brought happiness to the little bride but those stolen ones in which she and her husband were wont to take long walks together, sometimes into the country, again through the mazes of the great capital. Even at these times of respite she was only too well aware how Kano and the old nurse sat together at home, lamenting the gross selfishness of the young,—deciding, perhaps, upon the next loved painting or household treasure to be sold for buying rice. Tatsu, now as unreasonable and obstinate as Kano himself, still refused to admit unhappiness or threatened destitution. He and Umè-ko could go to the mountains, he said. "The mountains were, after all, their true home. Once there the Sennin and the deities of cloud would see that they did not suffer."

On an afternoon very near the end of the month the young couple took such a walk together. Their course lay eastward, crossing at right angles the main streets of the great city, until they reached the shores of the Sumida River, winding down like a road of glass. They had emerged into the famous district of Asakusa, where the great temple of Kwannon the Merciful attracts daily its thousands of worshippers. Here the water course is bounded by fashionable tea-houses, many stories high, and here the great arched bridges are always crowded. Leaving this busy heart of things, they sauntered northward, finding lonelier shores, and soon wide fields of green, until they reached a bank whereon grew a single leaning willow. The body of this tree, bending outward, sent its long, nerveless leaves in a perpetual green rain to the surface of the stream, where sudden swarms of minnows, like shivers in a glass, assailed the deceptive bait. The roots of the tree—great yellowish, twisted ropes of roots—clutched air, earth, and water in their convolutions. Among them the current, swifter here than in mid-stream, uttered at times a guttural, uncanny sound as of spectral laughter.

Umè-ko stood, one slender arm about the trunk, looking out, with mournful eyes, upon the passing river show. On the farther bank grew a continuous wall of cherry trees in yellowing leaf, and above them glowed the first hint of the coming sunset. Rising against the sky a temple roof, tilted like the keel of a sunken vessel, cut sharp lines into the crimson light.

Tatsu flung himself full length upon the bank. He patted the soil with its springing grasses, and felt his heart flow out in love to it. Then he reached up, caught at the drifting gauze of Umè's sleeve, and made as if to pull her down. Umè clasped the tree more tightly.

"Tatsu," she said, "I implore you not to think always of me. Look, beloved, the thin white sails of the rice-boats pass, and, over yonder, children in scarlet petticoats dance beneath the trees."

"I have eyes but for my wife," said wilful Tatsu.

Umè-ko drew the sleeve away. She would not meet his smile. "Alas, shall I forever obscure beauty!"

"There is no beauty now but in you! You are the sacred mirror which reflects for me all loveliness."

"Dear lord, those words are almost blasphemy," said Umè, in a frightened whisper. "Look, now, beloved, the light of the sun sinks down. Soon the great moon will come to us."

"What care I for a distant moon, oh, Dragon Maid," laughed Tatsu.

Umè's outstretched arm fell heavily to her side. "Alas!" she said again. "From deepest happiness may come the deepest pain. You dream not of the hurt you give."

"I give no hurt at all that I cannot more than heal," cried Tatsu, in his masterful way. But Umè's lips still quivered, and she turned her face from him.

In the silence that followed, the water among the willow roots gave out a rush and gurgle, a sound of liquid merriment,—perhaps the laugh of a "Kappa" or river sprite, mocking the perplexities of men. Umè-ko leaned over instantly, staring down into the stream.

"Umè-ko leaned over instantly, staring down into the stream."
Page 170.

"Umè-ko leaned over instantly, staring down into the stream."

"How deep it is, and strong," she whispered, as if to her own thought "That which fell in here would be carried very swiftly out to sea."

Tatsu smiled dreamily upon her. In his delight at her beauty, the delicate poise of body with its long, gray drifting sleeves, he did not realize the meaning of her words. One little foot in its lacquered shoe and rose-velvet thong, crushed the grasses at the very edge of the bank. Suddenly the earth beneath her shivered. It parted in a long black fissure, and then sank, with sob and splash, into the hurrying water. Umè tottered and clung to the tree. Tatsu, springing up at a single bound, caught her back into safety. The very branches above them shook as if in sentient fear. Umè felt herself pressed,—welded against her husband's side in such an agony of strength that his beating heart seemed to be in her own body. She heard the breath rasp upward in his throat and catch there, inarticulate. He began dragging her backward, foot by foot. At a safe distance he suddenly sank—rather fell—to earth bearing her with him, and began moaning over her, caressing and fondling her as a tiger might a rescued cub.

"Never go near that stream again!" he said hoarsely, as soon as he could speak at all. "Hear me, Umè-ko, it is my command! Never again approach that tree. It is a goblin tree. Some dead, unhappy woman, drowned here in the self-death, must inhabit it and would entice you to destruction. Oh, Umè, my wife,—my wife! I saw the black earth grinning beneath your feet. I cannot bear it! Come away from this place at once,—at once! The river itself may reach out snares to us."

"Yes, lord, I will come," she panted, trying to loosen the rigid arms, "but I am faint. This high bank is safe, now. And, lord, when you so embrace and crush me my strength does not return."

Tatsu grudgingly relaxed his hold. "Rest here then, close beside me," he said. "I shall not trust you, even an inch from me."

The river current in the tree roots laughed aloud.

Across and beyond the road of glass, the sky grew cold now and blue, like the side of a dead fish. A glow subtle and unmistakable as perfume tingled up through the dusk.

"The Lady Moon," whispered Umè, softly. Freeing her little hands she joined them, bent her head, and gave the prayer of welcome to O Tsuki Sama.

Tatsu watched her gloomily. "I pray to no moon," he said. "I pray to nothing in this place."

A huge coal barge on its way to the Yokohama harbor glided close to them along the dark surface of the tide. At the far end of the barge a fire was burning, and above it, from a round black cauldron, boiling rice sent up puffs of white, fragrant steam. The red light fell upon a ring of faces, evidently a mother and her children; and on the broad, naked back of the father who leaned far outward on his guiding pole. Umè turned her eyes away. "I think I can walk now," she said.

Tatsu rose instantly, and drew her upward by the hands. A shudder of remembered horror caught him. He pressed her once more tightly to his heart. "Umè-ko, Umè-ko, my wife,—my Dragon Wife!" he cried aloud in a voice of love and anguish. "I have sought you through the torments of a thousand lives. Shall anything have power to separate us now?"

"Nothing can part us now, but—death," said Umè-ko, and glanced, for an instant, backward to the river.

Tatsu winced. "Use not the word! It attracts evil."

"It is a word that all must some day use," persisted the young wife, gently. "Tell me, beloved, if death indeed should come—?"

"It would be for both. It could not be for one alone."

"No, no!" she cried aloud, lifting her white face as if in appeal to heaven. "Do not say that, lord! Do not think it! If I, the lesser one, should be chosen of death, surely you would live for our father,—for the sake of art!"

"I would kill myself just as quickly as I could!" said Tatsu, doggedly. "What comfort would painting be? I painted because I had you not."

"Because—you—had—me—not," mused little Umè-ko, her eyes fixed strangely upon the river.

"Come," said Tatsu, rudely, "did I not forbid you to speak of death? Too much has been said. Besides, the fate of ordinary mortals should have no potency for such as we. When our time comes for pause before rebirth we shall climb together some high mountain peak, lifting our arms and voices to our true parents, the gods of storm and wind. They will lean to us, beloved,—they will rush downward in a great passion of joy, catching us and straining us to immortality!"

By this they were from sight and hearing of the river, and had begun to thread the maze of narrow city streets in which now lamps and tiny electric bulbs and the bobbing lanterns of hurrying jinrikisha men had begun to twinkle. In the darker alleys the couple walked side by side. Umè, at times, even rested a small hand on her husband's sleeve. In the broad, well-lighted thoroughfares he strode on some paces in advance while Umè followed, in decorous humility, as a good wife should. Few words passed between them. The incident at the willow tree had left a gloomy aftermath of thought.

In the Kano home the simple night meal of rice, tea, soup, and pickled vegetables was already prepared. Mata motioned them to their places in the main room where old Kano was already seated, and served them in the gloomy silence which was part of the general strain. Throughout the whole place reproach hung like a miasma.

This evening, almost for the first time, Tatsu reflected, in full measure, the despondency of his companions. The elder man, glancing now and again toward him, evidently restrained with difficulty a flow of bitter words. Once he spoke to his daughter, fixing sunken eyes upon her. "The crimson lacquered wedding-chest that was your mother's, to-day has been sold to buy us food." Umè clenched her little hands together, then bowed far over, in token that she had heard. There were no words to say. For weeks now they had lived upon such money as this,—namida-kane,—"tear-money" the Japanese call it.

Tatsu, helpless in his place, scowled and muttered for a moment, then rose and hurried out, leaving the meal unfinished. Umè watched him sadly, but did not follow. This was so unusual a thing that Tatsu, alone in their chamber, was at first astonished, then alarmed. For ten minutes or more he paced up and down the narrow space, pride urging him to await his wife's dutiful appearance. In a short while more he felt the tension to be unbearable. A sinister silence flooded the house. He hurried back to the main room to find that Umè and old Kano were not there. He began searching the house, all but the kitchen. Instinctively he avoided old Mata's domain, knowing it to be the lair of an enemy. At last necessity drove him to it also. Her face leered at him through a parted shoji. He gave a bound in her direction. Instantly she had slammed the panels together; and before he could reopen them had armed herself with a huge, glittering fish-knife. "None of your mountain wild-cat ways for me!" she screamed.

In spite of wretchedness and alarm the boy laughed aloud. "I wish not to hurt you, old fool," he said. "I desire nothing but to know where my wife is."

"With her father," snapped the other.

"Yes, but where,—where? And why did she go without telling me? Where did he take her? Answer quickly. I must follow them."

"I have no answers for you," said Mata. "And even if I had you would not get them. Go, go, out of my sight, you Bearer of Discord!" she railed, feeling that at last an opportunity for plain speaking had arrived. "This was a happy house until your evil presence sought it. Don't glare at me, and take postures. I care neither for your tall figure nor your flashing eyes. You may bewitch the others, but not old Mata! Oh, Dragon Painter! Oh, Dragon Painter! The greatest since Sesshu!" she mimicked, "show me a few of the wonderful things you were to paint us when once you were Kano's son!

Bah! you were given my nursling, as a wolf is given a young fawn,—that was all you wanted. You will never paint!"

"Tell me where she is or I'll—" began the boy, raving.

"No you won't," jeered Mata, now in a transport of fury. "Back, back, out of my kitchen and my presence or this knife will plunge its way into you as into a devil-fish. Oh, it would be a sight! I have no love for you!"

"I care not for your love, old Baba, old fiend, nor for your knife. Where did my Umè go? You grin like an old she-ape! Never, upon my mountains did I see so vicious a beast."

"Then go back to your mountains! You are useless here. You will not even paint. Go where you belong!"

"The mountains,—the mountains!" sobbed the boy, under his breath. "Yes, I must go to them or my soul will go without me! Perhaps the kindlier spirits of the air will tell me where she is!" With a last distracted gesture he fled from the house and out into the street. Mata listened with satisfaction as she heard him racing up the slope toward the hillside. "I wish it were indeed a Kiu Shiu peak he climbed, instead of a decent Yeddo cliff," she muttered to herself, as she tied on her apron and began to wash the supper dishes. "But, alas, he will be back all too soon, perhaps before my master and Miss Umè come down from the temple."

In this surmise the old dame was, for once, at fault. Tatsu did not return until full daylight of the next morning. He had been wandering, evidently, all night long among the chill and dew-wet branches of the mountain shrubs. His silken robe was torn and stained as had been the blue cotton dress, that first day of his coming. At sight of his sunken eyes and haggard look Umè-ko's heart cried out to him, and it was with difficulty that she restrained her tears. But she still had a last appeal to make, and this was to be the hour.

In response to his angry questions, she would answer nothing but that she and her father had business at the temple. More than this, she would not say. As he persisted, pleading for her motives in so leaving him, and heaping her with the reproaches of tortured love, she suddenly threw herself on the mat before him, in a passion of grief such as he had not believed possible to her. She clasped his knees, his feet, and besought him, with all the strength and pathos of her soul, to make at least one more attempt to paint. He, now in equal torment, with tears running along his bronzed face, confessed to her that the power seemed to have gone from him. Some demon, he said, must have stolen it from him while he slept, for now the very touch of a brush, the look of paint, frenzied him.

Umè-ko went again to her father, saying that she again had failed. The strain was now, indeed, past all human endurance. The little home became a charged battery of tragic possibilities. Each moment was a separate menace, and the hours heaped up a structure already tottering.

At dawn of the next day, Tatsu, who after a restless and unhappy night had fallen into heavy slumber, awoke, with a start, alone. A pink light glowed upon his paper shoji; the plum tree, now entirely leafless, threw a splendid shadow-silhouette. At the eaves, sparrows chattered merrily. It was to be a fair day: yet instantly, even before he had sprung, cruelly awake, to his knees, he knew that the dreaded Something was upon him.

On the silken head-rest of Umè's pillow was fastened a long, slender envelope, such as Japanese women use for letters. Tatsu recoiled from it as from a venomous reptile. Throwing himself face down upon the floor he groaned aloud, praying his mountain gods to sweep away from his soul the black mist of despair that now crawled, cold, toward it. Why should Umè-ko have left him again, and at such an hour? Why should she have pinned to her pillow a slip of written paper? He would not read it! Yes, yes,—he must,—he must read instantly. Perhaps the Something was still to be prevented! He caught the letter up, held it as best he could in quivering hands, and read:

Because of my unworthiness, O master, my heart's beloved, I have been allowed to come between you and the work you were given of the gods to do. The fault is all mine, and must come from my evil deeds in a previous life. By sacrifice of joy and life I now attempt to expiate it. I go to the leaning willow where the water speaks. One thing only I shall ask of you,—that you admit to your mind no thought of self-destruction, for this would heavily burden my poor soul, far off in the Meido-land. Oh, live, my beloved, that I, in spirit, may still be near you. I will come. You shall know that I am near,—only, as the petals of the plum tree fall in the wind of spring, so must my earthly joy depart from me. Farewell, O thou who art loved as no mortal was ever loved before thee.

Your erring wife,
Umè-ko.

In his fantastic night-robe with its design of a huge fish, ungirdled and wild of eyes, Tatsu rushed through the drowsy streets of Yeddo. The few pedestrians, catching sight of him, withdrew, with cries of fear, into gateways and alleys.

At the leaning willow he paused, threw an arm about it, and swayed far over like a drunkard, his eyes blinking down upon the stream. Umè-ko's words, at the time of their utterance scarcely noted, came now as an echo, hideously clear. "That which fell here would be carried very swiftly out to sea." His nails broke against the bark. She,—his wife,—must have been thinking of it even then, while he,—he,—blind brute and dotard—sprawled upon the earth feeding his eyes of flesh upon the sight of her. But, after all, could she have really done it? Surely the gods, by miracle, must have checked so disproportionate a sacrifice! Suddenly his wandering gaze was caught and held by a little shoe among the willow roots. It was of black lacquer, with a thong of rose-colored velvet. With one cry, that seemed to tear asunder the physical walls of his body, he loosed his arm and fell.

IX

His body was found some moments later by old Kano and a bridge keeper. It was caught among the pilings of a boat-landing several hundred feet farther down the tide. A thin, sluggish stream of blood followed it like a clue, and, when he was dragged up upon the bank, gushed out terribly from a wound near his temple. He had seized, in falling, Umè-ko's lacquered geta, and his fingers could not be unclasped. In spite of the early hour (across the river the sun still peered through folds of shimmering mist) quite a crowd of people gathered.

"It is the newly adopted son of Kano Indara," they whispered, one to another. "He is but a few weeks married to Kano's daughter, and is called 'The Dragon Painter.'"

The efficient river-police summoned an ambulance, and had him taken to the nearest hospital. Here, during an entire day, every art was employed to restore him to consciousness, but without success. Life, indeed, remained. The flow of blood was stopped, and the wound bandaged, but no sign of intelligence awoke.

"It is to be an illness of many weeks, and of great peril," answered the chief physician that night to Kano's whispered question. The old man turned sorrowfully away and crept home, wondering whether now, at this extremity, the gods would utterly desert him.

Mata, prostrated at first by the loss of her nursling, soon rallied her practical old wits. She went, in secret, to the hospital, demanded audience of the house physician, and gave to him all details of the strange situation which had culminated in Umè's desperate act of self-renunciation, and induced Tatsu's subsequent madness. She did not ask for a glimpse of the sick man. Indeed she made no pretence of kindly feeling toward him, for, in conclusion, she said, "Now, August Sir, if, with your great skill in such matters, you succeed in giving back to this young wild man the small amount of intelligence he was born with, I caution you, above all things, keep from his reach such implements of self-destruction as ropes, knives, and poisons. Oh, he is an untamed beast, Doctor San. His love for my poor young mistress was that of a lion and a demon in one. He will certainly slay himself when he has the strength. Not that I care! His death would bring relief to me, for in our little home he is like the spirit of storm caged in a flower. Would I had never seen him, or felt the influence of his evil karma! But my poor old master still dotes on him, and, with Miss Umé vanished, if this Dragon Painter, too, should die at once, Kano could not endure the double blow!" The old woman began to sob in her upraised sleeve, apologizing through her tears for the discourtesy. The physician comforted her with kind words, and thanked her very sincerely for the visit. Her disclosures did, indeed, throw light upon a difficult situation.

From the hospital the old servant made her way to Uchida's hotel, to learn that he had gone the day before to Kiu Shiu. With this tower of strength removed Mata felt, more than ever, that Kano's sole friend was herself. The loss of Umè was still to her a horror and a shock. The eating loneliness of long, empty days at home had not yet begun; but Mata was to know them, also.

Kano, during the first precarious days of his son's illness, practically deserted the cottage, and lived, day and night, in the hospital. His pathetic old figure became habitual to the halls and gardens near his son. The physicians and nurses treated him with delicate kindness, forcing food and drink upon him, and urging him to rest himself in one of the untenanted rooms. They believed the deepening lines of grief to be traced by the loss of an only daughter, rather than by this illness of a newly adopted son. In truth the old man seldom thought of Umè-ko. He was watching the life that flickered in Tatsu's prostrate body as a lost, starving traveller watches a lantern approaching over the moor. "The gods preserve him,—the gods grant his life to the Kano name, to art, and the glory of Nippon," so prayed the old man's shrivelled lips a hundred times each day.

After a stupor of a week, fever laid hold of Tatsu, bringing delirium, delusion, and mad raving. At times he believed himself already dead, and in the heavenly isle of Ho-rai with Umè. His gestures, his whispered words of tenderness, brought tears to the eyes of those who listened. Again he lived through that terrible dawn when first he had read her letter of farewell. Each word was bitten with acid into his mind. Again and again he repeated the phrases, now dully, as a wearied beast goes round a treadmill, now with weeping, and in convulsions of a grief so fierce that the merciful opiate alone could still it.

The fever slowly began to ebb. For him the shores of conscious thought lay scorched and blackened by memory. More unwillingly than he had been dragged up from the river's cold embrace was he now held back from death. His first lucid words were a petition. "Do not keep me alive. In the name of Kwannon the Merciful, to whom my Umè used to pray, do not bind me again upon the wheel of life!" Although he fought against it with all the will power left to him, strength brightened in his veins. Stung into new anguish he prayed more fervently, "Let me pass now! I cannot bear more pain. I'll die in spite of you. Oh, icy men of science, you but give me the means with which to slay myself! I warn you, at the first chance I shall escape you all!"

"Mad youth, it is my duty to give you back your life even though you are to use it as a coward," said the chief physician.

Once when his suffering had passed beyond the power of all earthly alleviation, and it seemed as if each moment would fling the shuddering victim into the dark land of perpetual madness, Kano urged that the venerable abbot from the Shingon temple on the hill be summoned. He came in full regalia of office,—splendid in crimson and gold. With him were two acolytes, young and slender figures, also in brocade, but with hoods of a sort of golden gauze drawn forward so as to conceal the faces within. They bore incense burners, sets of the mystic vagra, and other implements of esoteric ceremony. The high priest carried only his tall staff of polished wood, tipped with brass, and surmounted by a glittering, symbolic design, the "Wheel of the Law," the hub of which is a lotos flower.

Tatsu, at sight of them, tossed angrily on his bed, railing aloud, in his thin, querulous voice, and scoffing at any power of theirs to comfort, until, in spite of himself, a strange calm seemed to move about him and encircle him. He listened to the chanted words, and the splendid invocations, spoken in a tongue older than the very gods of his own land, wondering, the while, at his own acquiescence. Surely there was a sweet presence in the room that held him as a smile of love might hold. He was sorry when the ceremony came to an end. The abbot, whispering to the others, sent all from the room but himself, Tatsu, and the smaller of the acolytes, who still knelt motionless at the head of the sick man's couch, holding upward an incense burner in the shape of a lotos seed-pod. The blue incense smoke breathed upward, sank again as if heavy with its own delight, encircling, almost as if with conscious intention, the kneeling figure, and then moved outward to Tatsu and the enclosing walls.

"My son," began the abbot, leaning gently over the bed, "I have a message from—her—"

"No, no," moaned the boy, his wound opening anew. "Do not speak it. I was beginning to feel a little peace from pain. Do not speak of her. You can have no message."

"I have known Kano Umè-ko her whole life long," persisted the holy man. "She is worthy of a nobler love than this you are giving her."

"There may be love more noble, but none—none—more terrible than mine," wailed out the sick man. "I cannot even die. I am quickened by the flames that burn me; fed by the viper, Life, that feeds on my despair.

My flesh cankers with a self-renewing sore! Could I but bathe my wounds in death!"

"Poor suffering one, this flesh is only the petal fallen from a perfected bloom! Whether her tender body, or this racked and twitching frame upon your bed, all flesh is illusion. Think of your soul and its immortal lives! Think of your wife's pure soul, and for its sake make effort to defy and vanquish this demon of self-destruction."

"Was not her own deed that of self-destruction?" challenged Tatsu, his sunken eyes set in bitter triumph upon the abbot. "I shall but go upon the road she went."

"To compare your present motives with your wife's is blasphemy," cried the other. "Her deed held the glory of self-sacrifice, that you might gain enlightenment; while you, railing impotently here, giving out affront against the gods, are as the wild beast on the mountain that cannot bear the arrow in its side."

"And it is true," said Tatsu, "I cannot bear the arrow,—I cannot endure this pain. Show me the way to death, if you have true pity. Let me go to her who waits me in the Meido-land."

"She does not wait you there, oh, grief deluded boy," then said the priest. "The message that I brought is this: bound still to earth by her great love for you her soul is near you,—in this room,—now, as I speak, seeking an entrance to your heart, and these wild railings hold her from you."

Tatsu half started from his pillow, and sank back. "I believe you not. You trick me as you would a child," he moaned.

The priest knelt slowly by the bed. "In the name of Shaka,—whom I worship,—these words of mine are true. Here, in this room, at this moment, your Umè-ko is waiting."

"But I want her too," whispered the piteous lips. "Not only her aerial spirit! I want her smile,—her little hands to touch me, the golden echo of her laughter,—I want my wife, I say! Oh, you gods, demons, preta of a thousand hells!" he shrieked, springing to a sitting posture in his bed, and beating the air about him with distracted hands. "These are the memories that whir down and close about me in a cloud of stinging wasps! I cannot endure! In the name of Shaka, whom you worship, strike me dead with the staff you hold,—then will I bless you and believe!" In a transport of madness, he leaned out, clutching at the staff, clawing down the stiff robes from the abbot's throat, snarling, praying, menacing with a vehemence so terrible, that the little acolyte, flinging down the still-burning koro, screamed aloud for help.

It was many hours before the nurses and physicians could quiet this last paroxysm. Exhaustion and a relapse followed. The long, dull waiting on hope began anew. After this no visitor but Kano was allowed. He entered the sick chamber only at certain hours, placing himself near the head of the bed where Tatsu need not see him. He never spoke except in answer to questions addressed him directly by his son, and these came infrequently enough. With this second slow return to vitality, Tatsu's most definite emotion seemed to be hatred of his adopted father. He writhed at the sound of that timid, approaching step, and dreaded the first note of the deprecating voice.

Kano was fully aware of this aversion. He realized that, perhaps, it would be better for Tatsu if he did not come at all; yet in this one issue the selfishness of love prevailed. Age and despair were to be kept at bay. He had no weapons but the hours of comparative peace he spent at Tatsu's bedside. Full twenty years seemed added to the old man's burden of life. His back was stooped far over; his feet shuffled along the wooden corridors with the sound of the steps of one too heavily burdened. He never walked now without the aid of his friendly bamboo cane. The threat of Tatsu's self-destruction echoed always in his ears. Away from the actual presence of his idol it gnawed him like a famished wolf, and his mind tormented itself with fantastic and dreadful possibilities. Once Tatsu had hidden under his foreign pillow the china bowl in which broth was served. Kano whispered his discovery to the nurse, and when she wondered, explained to her with shivering earnestness that it was undoubtedly the boy's intention to break it against the iron bedstead the first moment he was left alone, and with a shard sever one of his veins. Tatsu grinned like a trapped badger when it was wrested from him, and said that he would find a way in spite of them all. After this not even a medicine bottle was left in the room, and the watch over the invalid was strengthened.

"But," as old Kano remonstrated, "even though we prevent him for a few weeks more, how will it be when he can stand and walk,—when he is stronger than I?" To these questions came no answer. The second convalescence, so eagerly prayed for, became now a source of increasing dread. Something must be done,—some way to turn his morbid thoughts away from self-destruction. The old man climbed often, now, to the temple on the hill.

The hospital room, in an upper story, was small, with matted floors, and a single square window to the east. The narrow white iron bed was set close to this window, so that the invalid might gaze out freely. Tatsu did not ask that it be changed though, indeed, each recurrent dawn brought martyrdom to him. The sound of sparrows at the eaves, the smell of dew, the look of the morning mist as it spread great wings above the city, hovering for an instant before its flight, the glow of the first pink light upon his coverlid, each was an iron of memory searing a soul already faint with pain. The attendant often marvelled why, at this hour, Tatsu buried his face from sight, and, emerging into clearer day, bore the look of one who had met death in a narrow pass.

At noon, when the window showed a square of turquoise blue, he grew to watch with some faint pulse of interest the changing hues of light, and the clouds that shifted lazily aside, or heaped themselves up into rounded battlements of snow. Quite close to the window a single cherry branch, sweeping downward, cut space with a thick, diagonal line. Silvery lichens frilled the upper surface of the bark, and at the tip of each leafless twig, brown buds—small armored magazines of beauty—hinted already of the spring's rebirth. Life was all about him, and he hated life. Why should cherry blooms and sparrows dare to come again,—why should that old man near him wheeze and palpitate with life, why—why—should he, Tatsu, be held from his one friend, Death, when she, the essence of all life and beauty,—she who should have been immortal,—drifted alone, helpless, a broken white sea-flower, on some black, awful tide?

In the midst of such dreary imaginings, old Kano, late in the last month of the year, crept in upon his son. He was an hour earlier than his custom. Also there was something unusual,—a new energy, perhaps a new fear, noticeable in face and voice. But Tatsu, still bleeding with his visions of the dawn, saw nothing of this. The premature visit irritated him. "Go, go," he cried, turning his face sharply away. "This is a full hour early. Am I to have no moments to myself?"

"My son, my son," pleaded the old man, "I have come a little before time, because I have brought—"

"Do not call me son," interrupted the petulant boy. "It is wretchedness to look upon you. She would be here now, but for you. You killed her! You drove her to it!"

"No, Tatsu, you wrong me! As I have assured you, and as her own words say,—she made the sacrifice from her own heart. It was that her presence obscured your genius, my son. She was unselfish and noble beyond all other women. She—went—for your sake—"

"For my sake!" jeered the other. "You mean, for the sake of the things you want me to paint! Well, I tell you again, I will neither live *nor* paint! Yes, that touches you. Human agony is nothing to your heart of jade. You would catch these tears I shed to mix a new pigment! You do not regret her. You would think the price cheap, if only I will paint. I hate all pictures! I curse the things I have done! Would that, indeed, I had the tongue of a dragon, that I might lick them from the silk!"

"Tatsu, my poor son, be less violent. I urge nothing! The gods must do with you as they will, but here is something—a letter—" Fumbling, with shaking fingers, in his long, black sleeve, he drew out a filmy, white rectangle. The look of it, so like to one pinned to a certain pillow in the dawn, sent a new thrill of misery through the boy.

"A letter! Who would write me a letter,—unless souls in the Meido-land can write! Back, back,—do not touch me, or ere I kill myself I will find strength to slay you first. I will drag you with me to the underworld, as I journey in searching for my wife, and fling your craven soul to devils, as one would fling offal to a dog! Speak not to me of painting, nor of her!"

At the sight of extra attendants hurrying in, Tatsu waved them to leave him, threw himself back, stark, upon the pillow, and closed his eyes so tightly that the wrinkles radiated in black lines from the corners. He panted heavily, as from a long race. His forehead twitched and throbbed with purple veins.

Flung down cruelly from the exhilaration which a moment before had been his, old Kano seated himself on a chair directly in sight of Tatsu's bed. The nurses stole away, leaving the two men together. Each remained motionless, except for hurried breathing, and the pulsing of distended veins. A crow, perched on the cherry branch outside the window, tilted a cold, inquisitive eye into the room.

Tatsu was the first to move. The reaction of excitement was creeping upon him, drawing the sting from pain. He turned toward his visitor and began to study, with an impersonal curiosity, the aspect of the pathetic figure. Kano was sitting, utterly relaxed, at the edge of the cane-bottomed foreign chair His head hung forward, and his lids were closed. For the first time Tatsu noted how scanty and how white his hair had grown; how thin and wrinkled the fine old face. Something akin to compassion rose warm and human in the looker's throat. He had opened his lips to speak kindly (it would have been the first gentle word since Umè's loss) when the sight of his name, in handwriting, on the letter, froze the very air about him, and held him for an instant a prisoner of fear. The envelope dangled loosely from Kano's fingers. On it was traced, in Umè-ko's beautiful, unmistakable hand, "For my beloved husband, Kano Tatsu."

"The letter, the letter," he cried hoarsely, pointing downward. "It is mine,—give it!"

Kano raised his head. The reaction of excitement was on him too, and it had brought for him a patient hopelessness. It did not seem to matter a great deal just now what Tatsu did or thought. He would never paint. That alone was enough blackness to fill a hell of everlasting night.

"Give it to me," insisted the boy, leaning far out over the bed. "Did you bring it only to torture me? Quick, quick,—it is mine!"

"I brought it to give, and you repulsed me. I had found it but this morning, in your painting room, pinned to a silken frame on which you had begun her picture! She must have put it there before—before—"

"If you have a shred of pity or of love for me, give it and go," gasped the boy.

Kano rose with slow dignity. "Yes, it is for you, and I will give it and leave, as you ask, if I can have your promise—"

"Yes, yes, I promise everything,—anything,—I will not strive to slay myself,—at least until after your return—"

"That is enough," said the old man, and with a sigh held the missive out. Tatsu snatched it through the air. The perfume of plum blossoms was stealing from it. Once alone he crushed the delicate tissue against eyes and lips and throat. He rolled upon the bed in agony, only to press again to his heart this balm of her written words. It seemed to him, then, that the letter might really have come from the Meido-land. Could it be true, as the old priest said, that her soul continually hovered near, waiting only for him to give it recognition? "Umè, Umè,—my wife! Come back to me!" he cried aloud in an agony so great that it should drag her backward through that dark shadow-world,—not only the phantom of what she was, but Umè-ko herself, with the flower-like body, and the smile of light. He opened the missive slowly, that not a shred should be torn, and spread the thin tissue smoothly on his foreign pillow.

"This, beloved, being the forty-ninth day,—the seven-times-seventh-day after my passing,—when souls of those departed are given special privilege to return to earth, I speak thus, dumbly, to my lord. Although the fingers tracing now these timid lines are not permitted to touch you, oh, believe that, as you read, I wait at the door of your heart. O thou who art so dear, give to me, I pray, a shelter and a habitation. Then, because of my great love, I shall be one with you, bringing you comfort and myself great blessedness. O thou, who art still my husband, I beseech you to realize that any act on your part of violence and self-destruction will hurl our lives apart to the full width of the ten existences; so that, through another thousand years of unfulfilment we shall be groping in the dark, like children who have lost their way, calling ever, each on the name of the other.

"The birds of the air know, when storms arise, where to find their nests. Even the fox has shelter in the hill. Shall the soul of Umè-ko seek and find no shelter? Send me not forth again in lonely travail! Open your heart to me, O thou who art loved as no man was ever loved before thee! Umè-ko."

Kano, listening at the door, thought that the boy had fainted. One nurse, then another, crept near. At last the old man, unable to endure the strain, peered through a crevice. He fell back instantly, pressing both hands upon his mouth to stifle the cry of joy. Tatsu alive, awake, with eyes opened wide, gazed upward smiling, as into the face of Buddha.

X

The New Year festival, Shogatsu, had come and gone: white-flower buds gleamed like pearls on the lichen-covered, twisted limbs of the old "dragon-plum" by Umè's chamber ledge, when Tatsu and his adopted father entered once more together the little Kano home. If the young husband had realized, all along, what this coming ordeal might mean, he had given no sign of it. Kano and the physicians feared for him. The last test, it was to be, of sanity and of endurance. The actual hour of departure from the hospital fell late in January. More than once before a day had been decreed, only to be postponed because of a sudden physical weakening—mysterious and apparently without cause—on the part of the patient.

"I will return with you as soon as I may," Tatsu had assured his father on the day of reading Umè's letter. "I will try to live, and even to paint. Only, I pray you, speak not the name of—her I have lost."

This promise was given willingly enough. Kano's chief difficulty now was to hide his growing happiness. It was much to his interest that the subject of Umè be avoided. Even a dragon painter from the mountains must know something of certain primitive obligations to the dead, and for Umè not even an ihai had been set up by that of her mother in the family shrine. When Tatsu learned this he would marvel, and probably be angry. If by his own condition of silence he were debarred from attacking Kano, so much the better for Kano.

It was this disgraceful and unheard-of negligence—a matter already of common gossip in the neighborhood—that added the last measure of bitterness to old Mata's grief. Was her master demented through sorrow that he so challenged public censure, and was willing to cast dishonor upon the name of his only child? Hour after hour in the lonely house did the old dame seek to piece together the broken edges of her shattered faith. The master had always been a religious man, over-zealous, she had thought, in minute observances. Yet now he was willing to neglect, to ignore, the very fundamental principles of social decency. Personally he had seemed wretched enough after Umè's loss. The kindly neighbors had at first marvelled aloud at his whitening hair and heavily burdened frame. Mata, pleased at the sympathy, did nothing to distract it; but in her heart she knew that it was Tatsu's illness, not his daughter's death, that bore upon old Kano like the winter snow upon his pines.

On that most sacred period of mourning, the seven-times-seventh day after "divine retirement," when the spirit is privileged to enter most closely into the hearts of those that pray, Mata had believed that, beyond doubt, the full ceremony would be held. Surely the sweet, wandering soul was now to be given its kaimyo, was to be soothed by prayer, and be refreshed by the ghostly essence of tea and rice and fruit, placed before its ihai upon the shrine! What must the dead girl's mother have been thinking all this time? Mata woke before the dawn to pray. Kano, too, was awake early. She hurried to him, her first words a petition. But, no, he had no thought, even on this day of all days, for his child. He was off without his breakfast, an hour earlier than usual, to the hospital, a letter in his hand. Mata literally fell upon her knees before him, importuning him for the honor of the family name, if not in love for Umè-ko, to give orders at the temple for the holding of religious ceremonies. But Kano, himself almost in tears, eager, excited, though obviously in quite another whirlpool of emotions, urged her to be patient just a little longer. "I think all will yet be well," he assured her. "I have some hope to-day!"

"All will yet be well!" mocked the old dame through clenched teeth, watching the bent old figure hurrying from her. "As if anything could ever again be well, with my young mistress dead, and not even her body recovered for burial!"

In spite of her dislike for Tatsu, the lonely woman found herself watching, with some impatience, for the day of his actual return. Successive postponements had fretted her, and sharpened curiosity. She had not seen him since his illness. Upon that January noon when his kuruma rolled slowly in under the gate-roof, followed by anxious Kano and one of the male nurses from the hospital, she had turned toward him the old look of resentment: but, instead of the brief and chilling glance she had thought to use, found herself staring, gaping, in amazement and incredulity. She did not believe, for the first moment, that the wreck she saw was Tatsu. This bowed and shrunken ghost of suffering,—this loose, pallid semblance of a man, the beautiful, defiant, compelling demigod of the mountains that had swept down upon them! No! sorrow could wreak miracles of the soul, but no such physical transformation as this!

She continued to watch furtively, in a sort of terror, the tall figure as it was assisted from the kuruma and led, shambling, through the house. The three moved on to the wing containing Umè's chamber, and the painting room. Mata heard the fusuma close gently, the nurse's voice give admonition to "keep his spirit strong for this last stress," heard old Kano falter, "Farewell, my son, no one shall disturb you in these rooms," and had barely time to regain her presence of mind as the two men, Kano and the nurse, entered her kitchen. The former spoke: "Mata, your young master is to remain, unmolested, in that part of the house. Do not offer him rice, or tea, or anything whatever. When he needs and desires it he will himself emerge and ask for food. Above all things, do not knock upon his fusuma or call his name. These are the physician's orders."

"Exactly!" corroborated the nurse, with a professional air.

"Kashikomarimashita!" muttered the old dame in sullen acquiescence. "You need not have feared that I should intrude upon him!"

For three days and nights Tatsu remained to himself. The anxious listeners heard at times the sound of restless pacing up and down,—the thin, sibilant noise of stockinged feet sliding on padded straw. Again there would be a thud, as of a body fallen, or sunken heavily to the floor. Kano, on the second day, pale with apprehension, went early to the hospital for a revocation, or at least a modification of the instructions. The doctor's mandate was the same, "Do not go near him. Life, as well as reason, may depend upon this battle with his own despair. Only the gods can help him." To the gods, then, Kano went as well; climbing the long, steep road to the temple, where he made offerings and poured out from his anxious heart the very essence of loving prayer.

On the third day, Kano being thus absent, and old Mata alone in her kitchen as nervous, she would have told you, as a fish with half its scales off, she heard the fusuma of the distant room shudder, and then, with a sound of feeble jerks, begin to separate. She knew that it was Tatsu, and rallied herself for the approach. Through the shaded corridor came a figure scarcely animate, moving it would seem in answer to a soundless call. It entered the kitchen halting, and looking about as one in an unfamiliar place. On a square stone brasier, fed with glowing coals, the rice-pot steamed. The delicate vapor, tinged with aroma of the cooking food, made a fine mist in the air. Suddenly he thrust an arm out toward the fire. "Rice!—I am faint with hunger," he whispered. As if the few words had taken his last store of strength, he sank to the floor. Mata sprang to him. He had swooned. His face, young and beautiful in spite of the centuries of pain upon it, lay back, helpless, on her arm. She stared strangely down upon him, wondering where the old antipathy had gone, and striving (for she was an obstinate old soul, was Mata) consciously to recall it,—but the core of her hate was gone. Like a true woman she began to make self-excuses for the change. "It may have been because of this poor boy and his unhappy karma that my nursling had to die," said she. "But, look what love has done to him! Death is only another name for paradise compared with the agony sunken deep into this young face!"

She placed him gently, at full length, upon the padded floor. She chafed the flaccid wrists, the temples, the veins about his ears, and then, leaning over, blew on the heavy lids. "Umè-ko, my wife, my wife," he whispered, and tried to smile.

A wave of pity swept from the old dame's mind the last barrier of mistrust. "Yes, Master, here is Umè's nurse," she said in soothing tones. "Not Umè-ko,—she has gone away from us,—but the poor old nurse who loves her. I will serve you for her sake. Here, put your head upon this pillow,—she has often used it,—and now lie still until old Mata brings you rice and tea." She bustled off, her hands clattering busily among the cups and trays. As she worked, thankful, through her great agitation, for the familiar offices, she fought down, one by one, those great, distending sobs that push so hard a way upward through wrinkled throats.

Tatsu was still a little dazed. His eyes followed her about the room with a plaintive regard, as if not entirely sure that she was real. "Did you say that you were—Umè's—nurse," he asked.

"Yes. Don't you remember me, Master Tatsu? I am Mata, the old servant, and your Umè's nurse. I—I—was not always kind to you, I fear. I opposed your marriage, fearing for her some such sorrow as that which came. But it is past. The gods allowed it. I will now, for her sake, love and serve you,—my true master you shall be from this day, because I can see that your heart is gnawed forever by that black moth, grief, as mine is. Old Kano does not grieve,—he is a man of stone, of mud!" she cried. "But I must not speak of his sins, yet; here is the good tea, Master, and the rice." She fed him like a child, allowing, at first, but a single sip of tea, a grain or two of rice. He, in his weakness, was gentle and obedient, like a good child, eating all she bade him, and refraining when she told him that he had enough. It was a new Tatsu that sorrow had given to the Kano home.

But more wonderful than the transformation in him was, in Mata's thought, the complete reversal of her own emotions. Even in the midst of service she stopped to wonder how, so soon, it could be sweet to serve him,—to minister thus to the man she had called the evil genius of the house. In some mysterious way it seemed that through him the dead young wife was being served. In the smile he bent upon her, the old nurse fancied that she caught a tenderness as of Umè's smile. Perhaps, indeed, the homeless soul, denied its usual shelter in the shrine, made sanctuary of the husband's earthly frame. Perhaps, too, Kano had hoped for this, and so refused the ihai. However these high things might be, Mata knew she had gained strange comfort in the very fact of Tatsu's presence, in the companionship of his suffering.

When, being nourished, Tatsu insisted on sitting upright, and had recalled the scene about him, his first question was of Umè's shrine, where the ihai had been set, and what the kaimyo. This loosened Mata's tongue, and, with a sensation of deep relief, she began to empty her heart of its pent-up acrimony. Tatsu listened now, attentively; not as would have been his way three months before with gesticulations and frequent interruptions, but gravely, with consideration, as one intent to learn the whole before forming an opinion. Even at the end he would say nothing but the words, "Strange, strange; there must be a reason that you have not guessed."

"But we will get the ihai, will we not, Master? Together, when you are strong, we will climb the long road to the temple?" she questioned tremulously.

"Indeed we shall," said Tatsu, with his heartrending smile; "for at best, the thoughts of Kano Indara cannot be our thoughts. He let her die."

At this the other burst into such a passion of tears that she could not speak, but rocked, sobbing, to and fro, on the mats beside him. He wondered, with a feeling not far from envy, at this open demonstration of distress.

"I cannot weep at all," he said. Then, a little later, when she had become more calm, "Are your tears for me or for Umè-ko?"

"For both, for both," was the sobbing answer. "For her, that she had to die,—for you, that you must live."

"Both are things to weep for," said the boy, and stared out straight before him, as one seeing a long road.

Kano, returning later and finding the two together, marking as he did, at once, with the quick eye of love, how health already cast faint premonitions of a flush upon the boy's thin face, had much ado to keep from crying aloud his joy and gratitude. By strong effort only did he succeed in making his greeting calm. He used stilted, old-fashioned phrases of ceremony to one recently recovered from dangerous illness, and bowed as to a mere acquaintance. Tatsu, returning the bows and phrases, escaped in a few moments to his room, and emerged no more that day. Kano sighed a little, for the young face had been cold and stern. No love was to be looked for,—not yet, not yet.

For a few days Tatsu did nothing but lie on the mats; or wander, aimlessly, over the house and garden. He came whenever Mata summoned him to meals, and ate them with old Kano, observing all outer semblances of respect. But it seemed an automaton who sat there, eating, drinking, and then, at the last, bowing over to the exact fraction of an inch, each time, and moving away to its own rooms. The old artist, mindful of certain professional warnings from the hospital physicians, never spoke in Tatsu's presence of paintings, or of anything connected with art. Within a few days it seemed to him that Tatsu had begun to watch him keenly, as if expecting, every instant, the broaching of that subject which he knew was always uppermost in the other's mind. But the old man, for the first time in his whole life, had begun to use tact. He never followed Tatsu to his rooms, never intruded into those long conversations now held, many times a day, between Mata and her young master; never even commented to Mata upon her change of attitude. About five days after his first appearance in the kitchen, Tatsu and the old servant left the house together, giving Kano no hint of their destination. He watched them with a curious expression on his face. He knew that they were to climb together to the temple, and that it was a pilgrimage from which he was contemptuously debarred. They returned, some hours later, and were busied all the afternoon with the placing and decorations of an exquisite "butsu-dan," or Buddhist shelf, on which the ihai of the dead are placed. At the abbot's advice (and yet against all precedent) this was put, not beside the butsu-dan, where Kano's young wife had for so many years been honored, but in Tatsu's own bed-chamber, thus making of it a "mita-yama," or spirit room.

Kano, visiting it, unperceived, next day, noted with the same curious, half-quizzical, half-pathetic look that no Buddhist kaimyo or after-name had been given to his daughter. It was the earth-name, Kano Umè-ko, which the old abbot had written upon the lacquered tablet of wood. Added to it, as a sort of title, was the phrase, "To her who loves much." "That is true enough," thought old Kano, and touched his eyes an instant with his sleeve.

During the following week Tatsu, of himself, drew out his painting materials and tried to work. An instant later he had hurled the things from him with a cry, had slammed together the walls of his chamber, and lay in silence and darkness for many hours. At the time of the night-meal he came forth. Kano, to whom sorrow was teaching many things, made no comment upon his exclusion; and even old Mata refrained from searching his face with her keen eyes.

The next day he made the second attempt. His fusuma were opened, and Mata could see how his face blanched to yellow wax, how the lips writhed until they were caught back by strong, cruel teeth, and how the thin hands wavered. Notwithstanding this inward torture, he persisted. At first the lines of his brush were feeble. His work looked like that of a child.

Through subsequent days of discouragement and brave effort his power of painting grew with a slow but normal splendor of achievement. His fame began to spread. The "New Kano" and "The Dragon Painter of Kiu Shiu" the people of the city called him. Not only his work but his romantic, miserable story drew sympathy to him, and bade fair to make of him a popular idol. Older artists wished to paint his portrait. Print-makers hung about his house striving to catch at least a glimpse of him, which being elaborated, might serve as his likeness in the weekly supplement of some up-to-date newspaper. Sentimental maidens wrote poems to him, tied them with long, shining filaments of hair, and suspended them to the gate, or upon the bamboo hedges of the Kano home.

But against all these petty, personal annoyances Tatsu had the double guard of Kano and old Mata San. The pride of the latter in this "Son of our house" was unbounded. One would have thought that she discovered him, had rescued him from death and that it was now through her sole influence his reputation as an artist grew. Noble patrons came to the little cottage bearing rolls of white silk, upon which they entreated humbly, "That the illustrious and honorable young painter, Kano Tatsu, would some day, when he might not be augustly inconvenienced by so doing, trace a leaf or a cloud,—anything, in fact, that fancy could suggest, so that it was the work of his own inimitable hand. For the condescension they trusted that he would allow them to give a present of money,—as large a sum as he was willing to name."

"A second Sesshu! A second Sesshu!" old Kano would murmur to himself, in subdued ecstacy. "So did they load his ship with silk, four centuries ago!"

Of most of these commissions, Tatsu never heard. Kano did not wish the boy's work to be blown wide over the great city as it had been blown along the mountain slopes of Kiu Shiu. Nor did he wish the thought of gain or of personal ambition to creep into Tatsu's heart. Now he spent most of the day-lit hours secluded in his little study, painting those scenes and motives suggested by the keynote of his mood. Of late he had begun to read, with deep interest, the various essays on art, gathered in Kano's small, choice library. He would sometimes talk with his father about art, and let the eager old man demonstrate to him the different brush-strokes of different masters. The widely diversified schools of painting as they had flourished throughout the centuries of his country's social and religious life aroused in him an impersonal curiosity. He began to try experiments, realizing, perhaps, that to a genius strong and sane as his even fantastic ventures in technique were little more than bright images flecking, for an instant, the immutable surface of a mirror.

All methods were essayed,—the liquid, flowing line of the Chinese classics, Tosa's nervous, shattered lightning-strokes of painted motion, the soft, gray reveries of the great Kano school of three centuries before, when, to the contemplative mind all forms of nature, whether of the outer universe or in the soul of man, were but reflecting mirrors of a single faith; the heaped-up gold and malachite of Korin's decoration, sweet realistic studies of the Shijo school, even down to the horrors of "abura-yè," oil-painting, as it is practised in the Yeddo of to-day, each had for him its special interest and its inspiration. He leaned above the treasure-chests of time, choosing from one and then another, as a wise old jewel-setter chooses gems. Because ambition, art, existence had come to be, for him, gray webs spun thin across the emptiness of his days, because all hope of earthly joy was gone, he had now the power to trace, with almost superhuman mimicry and skill, the shadow-pictures of his shadow-world.

Yet gradually it became not merely a dull necessity to paint, the one barrier that held from him a devastating grief, but also something of a solace. The room where Umè's ever-lighted shrine was kept came more and more to seem the expression of herself. This the old priest had promised; Umè's letter had assured him that thus she would be near. In the blurred, purple hour of dusk when paints must be laid aside, and the heart given over to dreaming, the little room became her very earthly entity, the soft, smoke-tinted walls her breathing, the elastic matted floor but the remembered echoes of her feet, the sliding sliver fusuma her sleeves, the butsudan, with its small, clear lamp, its white wood, and its flowers, her face.

Now always he kept the walls that used to separate their chamber and his painting room removed; so that a single essence filled both rooms. And here, as he worked silently day after day, it seemed to him that she had learned to come. At first shy, undecided, in some far corner of the space she watched him; then, taking courage, would drift near. She leaned now by his shoulder, as he worked. Always it was the left shoulder. He could feel her breath—colder indeed than from a living woman—upon his bared throat. Sometimes a little hand, light as the dust upon a moth's wing, rested the ghost of a moment on his robe. Once, he could have sworn her cheek had touched his hair. So strong was this impression that an ague shivered through him, and his heart stopped, only to beat again with violent strokes. When the physical tremor was over he arose, took up her round metal mirror, and went to the veranda to see by strong light whether any trace of the spirit touch remained. No, there was only, as usual, the tossed, black locks of hair through which sorrow had begun to weave her silver strands.

January, with its snows, had passed. The plum-tree buds had opened, one by one, in the chill, early winds of spring, giving at times unwilling hospitality to flakes of snow whiter than themselves. In February, under warmer sunshine, the blossoms showed in constellations, a myriad on a single branch. Then, all too soon, the falling of wan petals made a perfumed tragedy of snow upon the garden paths.

Tatsu grew to love the old dragon plum as Umè-ko had loved it. She was its name-child, Umè, and he felt its sweetness to be one with her. At night the perfume crept in to him through crannies of the close-shut amado and shoji, revivifying, to keen agony, his longing for his wife. There were moonlit nights he could not rest for it, but would rise, pacing the cold, wet pebbles of the garden, or wandering, like a distracted spirit that had lost its way, through the thoroughfares of the sleeping town.

His whole life now, since he had cheated death, was blurred and vague. To himself he seemed an unreal thing projected, like a phantom light, upon the wavering umbra of two contrasting worlds. The halves of him, body and animating thought, fitted each other loosely, and had a strange desire to drift apart. The quiet, obedient Tatsu, regaining day by day the strength and beauty that his clean youth owed him, was to the inner Tatsu but a painted shell. The real self, clouded in eternal grief, knew clarity and purpose only before a certain flower-set shrine. He believed now, implicitly, that Umè's soul dwelt near him, was often with him in this room. A resolve half formed, and but partially admitted to himself,—for things of the other world are not well to meddle with,—grew slowly in him, to compel, by worship and never-relaxing prayer, the presence of her self,— her insubstantiate body, outlined upon the ether in pale light, or formed in planes of ghostly mist. Others had thus drawn visions from the underworld, and why not he?

Even now she was, for him, the one fact of the ten existences. She knew it and he knew it. Why should not sight be added to the unchallenged datum of the mind. Living, they had often read each other's thoughts. They held, he knew, as yet, their separate intelligences,—still they could bridge a blessed duality by love. Even now it would have surprised him little to hear the very sound of her voice echo from the inner shrine, to feel a little white hand pass like a cloud across his upraised brow. At such moments he told himself that he was satisfied, she was his until death and beyond. No one could separate them now!

These were, alas, the higher peaks of love. There waited for him, as he knew too well, steep hillsides set with swords, and valleys terrible with fire.

> "So that we be together,
> Even the Hell of the Blood Lake,
> Even the Mountain of Swords,
> Mean nothing to us at all!"

So they had sung. So that we be together! Ah, together,—that was the essence of it, that the key! "And this is what I want!" groaned the suffering man. "This ghostly resignation is a self-numbing of the heart. I care not for the ghost, the spirit, however pure. I want the wife I have lost,—her smile, her voice, her little hands to touch me! Oh, Umè-ko, my wife, my wife!" If, as the abbot said, this phase of grief were bestial, were unworthy of the woman who had died for him, then why did not the listening soul of her shrink? He knew that it was not repelled, whatever the frenzy of his grief. Indeed, at such times of agony she leaned down closer, longing to comfort him. If it were given her to speak she would have cried, "My husband!" Wherever she might drift,—in the black ocean, in the Meido-land, yes, even in the smile of Buddha on his throne,—she yearned for her lover as he for her, with a human love; she stretched out arms of mist to him, and tinged the pale ether of the spirit world with love's rosy flame.

One such night, during the time of plum-tree falling, when the boy, tortured by the almost human sweetness of the flowers, had risen from his bed to flee memory across the wide, cold plains of night, he had left, in his hurried going, the doors and shutters of his room spread wide. Mata and old Kano, accustomed to these midnight sounds, merely turned on their lacquered pillows, murmured "Poor tormented Tatsu," and went to sleep again. It had been a day of power for the young artist, but not a day of peace. The picture he had worked on he would have called one of his "nightmare fancies." It showed a slender form in gray with one arm about a willow. She and the tree both leaned above swift, flowing water, and her eyes were fixed in sombre brooding. On the bank, in abrupt foreshortening, lay the figure of a man. He looked at her. From the river, unmarked as yet by either, rose the gray face and long, red hair of a Kappa, or malicious river sprite. This sketch, unfinished, for the Kappa was a mere indication of red locks and a tall, thin form, stood against a pillar of the tokonoma at just the angle where the soft light of the butsu-dan shed a pale glow across it. Brushes, paints, and various small saucers littered the floor. Tatsu had stopped his work abruptly, overcome by the very power of his own delineation.

He was absent from the house for several hours. The long walk through unseen streets and over unnoticed bridges had given the boon, at least, of physical fatigue. Now, perhaps, he could get to sleep before the black ants of thought had rediscovered him. Entering the room quietly he closed the shoji, smoothed the bed-clothes with an impatient hand, and knelt, for an instant, before the shrine. Perhaps, after all, rest was not to come. The air was sweet and heavy with Umè-ko. The faint perfume of sandalwood which, living, always hung about her garments, flowed in with the odor of the plum. She must be near,—Umè herself, in mortal garments. In the next room, the veranda, hiding in the closet to spring out merrily upon him! He groaned and strove to plunge his mind into prayer.

The unfinished picture stood close at hand. Suddenly he noticed it, and, with a gasp, stooped to it. Something had changed; the whole vibration of its lines were subtly new. There was the girl's figure, the leaning willow, the man,—content, insensate, sprawling upon the bank,—but the Kappa!

Buddha the Merciful, could it be true? Where he had left a Kappa, waiting until to-morrow to give the triumph, the leering satisfaction at the human grief it fed on, rose the white form and pitying face of Kwannon Sama,— she to whom his Umè loved to pray. The eyes, soft, humid with compassion, looked directly out to his. They were Umè's eyes! He caught up one brush after the other. All had been used, and Umè's touch was upon them. Her aura permeated them.

He rushed now to the veranda. In leaving the rooms, three hours before, he had not taken the usual stone step which led into the garden under the branches of the plum, but had leaped directly from the low flooring, not caring where he trod. He remembered now that the stone had been white in the moonlight. It was now swept clean of petals, as though by the hurried trailing of a woman's dress. Was this the way in which she was to manifest herself? And would a spirit-robe brush surfaces so vehemently? And would a ghostly hand use brushes and pigments of ground-earth?

Unable to endure the room, he went again into the night, no further this time than the little garden. In the neighborhood dogs were barking fiercely, as though in the wake of a presence. By sound he followed it, and it moved up the hill. The very garden now was tinged with sandalwood.

Until the dawn, and after, he walked the pebbled paths, not thinking, indeed not fearing, hoping, or giving conscious form to speculation. He was dazed. But the young blood in his veins ran alternate currents of fire and ice.

With the first sun-ray he perceived a companion in the dewy solitude. He had noticed the figure before, but always, until this hour, at twilight. It was the form of a nun standing, high above him on the temple cliff, with one arm about a tree.

After this nothing mysterious broke the quiet routine of his life. The presence of Umè in the chamber seemed to fade a little, but, for some reason inexplicable to himself, this brought now no poignant grief. He did not tell the wonderful thing to Mata or old Kano, but hid the still unfinished picture where no one but himself could see it.

So February passed, and March.

XI

With April came the cherry-flowers, wistaria, and peonies; with iris in the bud, and shy hedge-violets; wonder of yama buki shrubs that played gold fountains on the hills, and the swift, bright contagion of young grass. Even from old Kano's moon-viewing hillock one might see, in looking out across the desert of gray city roofs, round tops of cherry trees rising like puffs of rosy smoke. From out the face of the temple cliff long, supple fronds of ferns unrolled, bending uncertain arms toward the garden. The tangled sasa-grass rustled new sleeves of silk; and the great camphor tree, air-hung in blue, seemed caught in a jewelled mesh of chrysoprase and gold.

Down in the lower level of the garden, too, springtime busied itself with beauty. The potted plants, once Umè-ko's loved charges, had become now, quite mysteriously to himself, Tatsu's companions and his special care. Among the more familiar growths a few foreign bushes had been given place, a rose, a heliotrope, and a small, frightened cyclamen. Slips of chrysanthemum needed already to be set for the autumn yield. Tatsu, watering and tending them, thought with wistful sadness upon these plans for future enjoyment. "We are all bound upon the wheel of life," he said to them. "Would that with me, as you, the turning were but for a single season!"

"My son," the elder man began abruptly, at a certain noonday meal about the middle of the month, "how is it that you never go with me to the temple on the hill?"

Tatsu looked up from his rice-bowl in some surprise. The relations between these two, though externally kind, had never approached intimacy. Kano indeed idolized his adopted son with pathetic and undisguised fervor; but with Tatsu, though other things might have been forgiven, the old man's continued disrespect to his daughter's memory, his refusal to join even in the simplest ceremony of devotion, kept both him and old Mata chilled and distant. The one possible explanation,—aside from that of wanton cruelty,—was a thing so marvellous, so terrible in implied suggestion, that the boy's faint soul could make for it no present home; let it drift, a great luminous nebula of hope, a little longer on the rim of nothingness.

The answer now to Kano's question betrayed a hint of the more rational animosity.

"You had never seemed to desire it. And I have my place of worship here."

"Yes, I know. Of course I knew that!" the other hurried on in some agitation. Then he paused, as if uncertain how to word the following thought. "I do wish it!" he broke forth, with an effort. "I make request now that you go with me, this very day, at twilight."

"If it is your honorable desire," said Tatsu, bowing in indifferent acquiescence. A moment later he had finished his meal, and rose to go.

Kano moved restlessly on the mats. He drew out the solace of a little pipe, but his nervous fingers fumbled and shook so, that the slim rod of bamboo tipped with silver escaped him, and went clattering down among the empty dishes of the tray. Mata's apprehensive face showed instantly at a parting of the kitchen fusuma. She sighed aloud, as she noted a great triangle chipped from the edge of an Imari bowl. Only two of those bowls had remained; now there was but one.

"Tatsu, my son, may I depend upon you? This day, as soon as the light begins to fail?"

Tatsu, in the doorway, paused to look. Evidently the speaker struggled with a strong excitement. Something in the twitching face, the eager, shifting eyes, brought back a vision of that meal on the evening that preceded Umè's death, when she and her father had leaned together, whispering, ignoring him, and afterward had left the house, giving him no hint of their errand. He felt with dread a premonition of new bitterness.

"I shall be ready at the twilight hour," he said, and went to his room.

That afternoon Tatsu did little painting. Silent and motionless as one of the frames against the wall, he sat staring for long intervals out upon the garden. The sunshine gave no pleasure, only a blurring of his sight. Beauty was not there for him, this day. He was thinking of those hours of October sunlight, when the whole earth reeled with joy, for Umè-ko was of it! Where was she now? And what had there been in Kano's look and voice to rouse those sleeping demons of despair? Could any new sorrow await him at the temple? No, his present condition had at least the negative value of absolute void. From nothing, nothing could be taken; and to it, nothing be supplied!

In spite of this colorless assurance it was with something of reluctance, of shrinking, that he prepared to leave the house. Few words were spoken between the two. Catching up the skirts of narrow, silken robes a little higher, they tucked the folds into their belts, and side by side began the long, slow climbing of the road.

The city roofs beneath them hurried off to the edge of the world like ripples left in the gray sand-bed of a stream. Above the plain the mist drew in its long, horizontal lines of gray.

About half the distance up the steep the temple bell above them sounded six slow, deliberate strokes. First came the sonorous impact of the swinging beam against curved metal, then the "boom," the echo,—the echoes of that echo to endless repetition, sifting in layers through the thinner air upon them, sweeping like vapor low along the hillside with a presence and reality so intense that it should have had color, or, at least, perfume; settling in a fine dew of sound on quivering ferns and grasses, permeating, it would seem, with its melodious vibration the very wood of the houses and the trunks of living trees.

Reaching at last the temple court, old Kano took the lead, crossed the wide-pebbled space, and halted with his companion at the edge of the cliff. A cry of wonder came from Tatsu's lips; that low, inimitable cry of the true artist at some new stab of beauty. Delicately the old man withdrew, and hid himself in the shadow of the temple.

Tatsu stared out, alone. He saw the round bay like a mirror,—like Umè's mirror; and to the west the peak of Fuji, a porphyry cone against the sunset splendor. No wonder that the gray nuns came here at this hour, or that she, the slender, isolated one, lingered to drain the last bright drop of beauty! He looked about now to discover her tree. Yes, there it was, quite close; not a willow as he had sometimes thought, but a young maple, unusually upright of growth. It had been leafless, but now the touch of spring had lighted every twig with a pale flame-point of red. He recalled that in the autumn it had made a crimson heart against the sky; and later had sent down into the Kano garden frail alms of ruby films. Umè had loved to catch them in her hands, wondering at their brightness, and trying to make him wonder, too. Love-letters of the passing year, she called them; songs dyed with the autumn's heart's-blood of regret that he must yield the sweet, warm earth to his gray rival, winter. She had pretended that the small, crossed veinlets of the leaves were Chinese ideographs which it was given her to decipher. Holding him off with one outstretched arm she would have read to him,—fantastic, exquisite interpreter of love,—but he, mad brute, had caught the little hands, the autumn leaves, and crushed them to one hot glow, crying aloud that nature, beauty, love were all made one in her. Such grief he must have given many times.

He threw his head back as in sudden hurt, a gesture becoming habitual to him, and drew a long, impatient, tremulous sigh. As if to cast aside black thought, he strode over quickly to the maple tree, flung an arm around it, and leaned over to stare down into his garden with the gray nun's eyes. There it was, complete, though in miniature;—rocks, pines, the pigmy pool, the hillock squatting in one corner like an old, gray garden toad, and in another corner, scarcely of larger size, the cottage.

Kano plucked nervously at his sleeve. "You lean too far. Come, Tatsu, I have a—a—place to show you."

Tatsu wheeled with a start. Try as he would he shivered and grew faint, even yet, at the sound of Kano's voice breaking abruptly in upon a silence. He gave a nod of acquiescence and, with downbent head, followed his guide diagonally across the temple court, past the wide portico where sparrows and pigeons fought for night-quarters in the carved, open mouths of dragons, along the side of the main building until, to Tatsu's wonder, they stopped before a little gate in the nunnery wall.

"I thought it was almost death for a man to enter here!" exclaimed the boy.

"For most men it is," said Kano, producing a key of hammered brass about nine inches long. "But I desired to go the short path to the cemetery, and it lies this way. As I have told you, the abbot was my boyhood's friend."

Within the convent yard,—a sandy space enclosed in long, low buildings of unpainted wood,—Tatsu saw a few gray figures hurrying to cover; and noticed that more than one bright pair of eyes peered out at them through bamboo lattices. Over the whole place brooded the spirit of unearthly peace and sweetness which had been within the gift of the holy bishop and his acolytes even at that time of torment in the hospital cell. The same faint Presence, like a plum tree blossoming in the dark, stole through the young man's senses, luring and distressing him with its infinite suggestions of lost peace.

At the farther wall of the court they came to an answering door. This was already unlocked and partially ajar. It opened directly upon the highest terrace of the cemetery which led down steeply in great, curved, irregular steps to a plain. The crimson light in the west had almost gone. Here to the north, where rice-fields and small huddled villages stretched out as far as the eye could see, a band of hard, white light still rested on the horizon, throwing back among the hillside graves a pale, metallic sheen. Each shaft of granite was thus divided, one upright half, blue shadow, the other a gray-green gleam. All looked of equal height. A gray stone Buddha on his lotos pedestal, or the long graceful lines of a standing Jizo, only served to emphasize the uniformity.

This was a place most dear to Kano, and had been made so to his child. He even loved the look of the tombs. "Gray, splintered stalagmites of memory," he had called them, and when the child Umé had learned the meaning of the simile she had put her little finger to a spot of lichen and asked, "Then are these silver spots our tears?"

The old man stepped down very softly to the second tier. A nightingale was calling low its liquid invocation, "Ho-ren-k-y-y-o-o-o!" Perhaps old Kano moved so softly that he might not lose the echoes of this cry. The two men seemed alone in the silent scene. Once Tatsu thought his eye caught a swift flicker, as of a gray sleeve, but he was not sure. At any rate he would not think of it, or speculate, or marvel! He was beginning to tremble before the unknown. The sense of shrinking, of miracle, of being, perhaps, too small to contain the thing decreed, bore hard upon him. With it came a keen impression of the unreality of the material universe,—of Buddhist illusion. Even these adamantine records of death, rising on every side to challenge him,—even these might recombine their particles before his very eyes,—might shiver into mist and float down to the plain to mingle with the smoke of cooking as it rose from the peasant huts. Anything might happen, or nothing!

Kano had stopped short before a grave. For once Tatsu was glad to hear his voice.

"Here lie the clean ashes of my young wife, Kano Uta-ko," said the old man, without preface or explanation.

"In former days, before—before my illness, I came here often," said the other. His eyes hung on the written words of the kaimyo. "If you grieved deeply, it must have been great solace that you could come thus to her grave," he added wistfully. Then, as Kano still remained silent, he read aloud the beautiful daishi, "A flower having blossomed in the night, the Halls of the Gods are Fragrant."

Kano drew a long sigh. "For nineteen years I have mourned her," he went on slowly. "As you know, a son was not given to us. She died at Umé's birth. I could not bring myself to replace her, even in the dear longing for a son."

"A son!" Tatsu knew well what the old man meant. He lifted his eyes and stared out, mute, into the narrowing band of light. The old man drew his thin form very straight, moved a few feet that he might look squarely into the other's face, and said deliberately. "So did I mourn the young wife whom I loved, and so, if I know men, will you mourn, Kano Tatsu. Of such enduring stuff will be your grief for Umè-ko."

It was said. The old man's promise had been torn like a leaf,—not to be mended or recalled,—torn and flung at his listener's feet. Yet such was the simplicity of utterance, such the nobility of poise, the beauty of the old face set like a silver wedge into the deepening mist, that Tatsu could only give him look for look, with no resentment. The young voice had taken on strangely the timbre of the old as, in equal soberness, he answered,

"Such, Kano Indara, though I be burdened with years as many as your own,—will be the never-ceasing longing for my lost wife, Umè-ko."

A little sob, loosed suddenly upon the night, sped past them. "What was it? Who is there?" cried Tatsu, sharply, wheeling round.

Kano began to shake. "Perhaps—perhaps a night-bird," he stammered out.

"A bird!" echoed Tatsu. "That sound was human. It is a woman, the Presence that has hung about me! Put down your arms,—you cannot keep me back!"

"Be still!" cried out old Kano in the voice of angry kings. "Nothing will happen,—nothing, I say, if you act thus like the untamed creature that you were! Your fate is still in my hands, Kano Tatsu!"

Tatsu fell down upon his knees, pulling at the old man's sleeves. "Father, father, have pity! I will be self-controlled and docile as I have been these long, long months. But now there is a thing so great that would possess me, my soul faints and sickens. Father, I ask your help, your tenderness. I think I have wronged you from the first,—my father!"

Suddenly the old man hurled his staff away and sank weeping into the stronger arms. "I fear, I fear!" he wailed. "It may be still too early. But she said not,—the abbot counselled it! O gods of the Kano home!"

"Father," asked Tatsu, rising slowly to his feet, his arms still close about the other, "can it be joy that is to find me, even in this life?"

"Wait, you shall see," cried the old man, now laughing aloud, now weeping, like a hysterical girl. "You shall see in a moment! My dead wife takes me by the hand and leads me from you,—just a little way, dear Tatsu, just here among the shadows. No longer are the shadows for you,—joy is for you. Yes, Uta-ko, I 'm coming. The young love springs like new lilies from the old. Stand still, my son; be hushed, that joy may find you."

He faltered backward and was lost. Upon the hillside came a stillness deeper than any previous interval of pause. From it the nightingale's low note thrust out a wavering clew. The day had gone, and a few stars dotted the vault of the sky. Tatsu threw back his head. There was no pain in the gesture now; he was trying to make room in his soul for an unspeakable visitor. The arch of heaven had grown trivial. Eternity was his one boundary. The stars twinkled in his blood.

He heard the small human sob again, just at his elbow. All at once he was frozen in his place; he could not turn or move. His arms hung to his sides, his throat stiffened in its upward lines. And then a little hand, stealing from a nun's gray sleeve, slipped into his, and in a pause, a hush, it was before the full splendor of love's cry, he turned and saw that it was Umè-ko, his wife.

"Then a little hand, stealing from a nun's gray sleeve, slipped into his." *Page* 259.

"Then a little hand, stealing from a nun's gray sleeve, slipped into his."

Yeddo and modern Tokyo alike give entertainment to the traditional nine days' wonder. Sometimes the wonder does not fade at all, and so it was with the case of Tatsu and his wife. If he had been an idol, he was now a demigod, Umè-ko sharing the sweet divinity of human tenderness with him.

Had it all happened a century before, the people would have built for them a yashiro, with altar and a shrine. Here they would have been worshipped as gods still in the flesh, and lovers would have prayed to them for aid and written verses and burned sweet incense.

Being of modern Tokyo, most of this adulation went into newspaper articles. Old men envied Kano his dutiful daughter, young men envied Tatsu his beautiful and loving wife. The print-makers, indeed, perpetrated a series of representations that put old Kano's artistic teeth on edge. First there was Umè at the willow; then Tatsu, in the same place, taking his mad plunge for death's oblivion; Umè, the hooded acolyte, kneeling in the sick chamber at the head of her husband's bed; Umè, the nun, standing each day at twilight on the edge of the temple cliff to catch a glimpse of him she loved; and, at the last, Tatsu and Umè rejoined beside the tomb of Kano Uta-ko. Fortunately these pictures were never seen by the two most concerned.

They went away on a second bridal journey, this time to Tatsu's native mountains in Kiu Shiu. While there, the good friend Ando Uchida was to be sought, and made acquainted with the strange history of the previous months.

Mata and her old master remained placidly at home. They had no fears. At the appointed date—only a week more now—the two would come back, as they had promised, to begin the long, tranquil life of art and happiness. There were to be great pictures! Kano chuckled and rubbed his lean hands together, as he sat in his lonely room. Then the thought faded, for a tenderer thought had come. In a year or more, if the gods willed, another and a keener blessedness might be theirs.

To dream quite delicately enough of this, the old man shut his eyes. Oh, it was a dream to make the springtime of the world stir at the roots of being! A tear crept down from the blue-veined lids, making its way through wrinkles, those "dry river-beds of smiles." If the baby fingers came,—those small, fearless fingers that were one's own youth reborn,—they would press out all fretful lines of age, leaving only tender traceries. He leaned forward, listening. Already he could hear the tiny feet echo along the rooms, could see small, shaven heads bowing their first good morning to the O Ji San,— revered, beloved patriarch of the home! How old Mata would idolize and scold and pet them! A queer old soul was Mata, with faults, as all women have, but in the main, a treasure! Good times were coming for the old folks in that house! So sat Kano, dreaming, in his empty chamber; and unless we have eternity to spare, nodding beside him on the mats, we must bow, murmuring, "Sayo-nara!"

CPSIA information can be obtained
at www.ICGtesting.com
Printed in the USA
LVHW052358021121
702257LV00007B/775